Count
Your
Blessings

BOOKS BY KENNETH W. OSBECK

25 Most Treasured Gospel Hymn Stories

52 Bible Characters Dramatized:
Easy-to-Use Monologues for All Occasions

101 Hymn Stories:
The Inspiring True Stories Behind 101 Favorite Hymns

101 More Hymn Stories:
The Inspiring True Stories Behind 101 Favorite Hymns

Amazing Grace:
366 Inspiring Hymn Stories for Daily Devotions

Count Your Blessings:
A Closer Look at 30 Hymns of Gratitude

Devotional Warm-Ups for the Church Choir:
Preparing to Lead Others in Worship

Let Us Break Bread Together:
A Closer Look at 30 Hymns About Fellowship

The Ministry of Music:
A Complete Handbook for the Music Leader in the Local Church

Hymn Stories & for Real Life

Count Your Blessings

A CLOSER LOOK AT 30 HYMNS OF GRATITUDE

KENNETH W. OSBECK
COMPILED AND EDITED BY JANYRE TROMP

FOREWORD BY SELAH

KREGEL
PUBLICATIONS

Count Your Blessings: A Closer Look at 30 Hymns of Gratitude
© 2024 by The Estate of Kenneth Osbeck

Compiled from Kenneth W. Osbeck's previously published works: *Amazing Grace: 366 Inspiring Hymn Stories for Daily Devotions* (Kregel, 2010); *101 Hymn Stories: The Inspiring True Stories Behind 101 Favorite Hymns* (Kregel, 2012, 2023); *101 More Hymn Stories: The Inspiring True Stories Behind 101 Favorite Hymns* (Kregel, 2013).

Published by Kregel Publications, a division of Kregel Inc., 2450 Oak Industrial Dr. NE, Grand Rapids, MI 49505. www.kregel.com.

Kenneth W. Osbeck's originally published hymn stories did not include source citations. However, the industry upholds Osbeck's works as credible sources, which are often cited as a primary source of information. We have done due diligence to find sources when possible and to include citations. For all other sources, we trust they can be found in Osbeck's selected bibliography, which we have included in this work.

We are grateful to PDHymns.org, Hymnary.org, and the Cyber Hymnal™ for providing sheet music for some of the public domain hymns included in this book.

All Scripture quotations, unless otherwise indicated, are taken from the Holy Bible, New International Version®, NIV®. Copyright © 1973, 1978, 1984, 2011 by Biblica, Inc.™ Used by permission of Zondervan. All rights reserved worldwide. www.zondervan.com. The "NIV" and "New International Version" are trademarks registered in the United States Patent and Trademark Office by Biblica, Inc.™ Scripture quotations marked ESV are from the ESV® Bible (The Holy Bible, English Standard Version®), copyright © 2001 by Crossway, a publishing ministry of Good News Publishers. Used by permission. All rights reserved. Scripture quotations marked NKJV are taken from the New King James Version®. Copyright © 1982 by Thomas Nelson. Used by permission. All rights reserved. Scripture quotations marked NLT are taken from the Holy Bible, New Living Translation, copyright ©1996, 2004, 2015 by Tyndale House Foundation. Used by permission of Tyndale House Publishers, Carol Stream, Illinois 60188. All rights reserved.

Cataloging-in-Publication Data is available from the Library of Congress.

ISBN 978-0-8254-4246-9, print
ISBN 978-0-8254-6375-4, epub
ISBN 978-0-8254-6374-7, Kindle

Printed in the United States of America
24 25 26 27 28 29 30 31 32 33 / 5 4 3 2 1

CONTENTS

Contents

FOREWORD

HELLO, FRIENDS!

I am so honored to write a foreword to this wonderful book by Mr. Kenneth Osbeck! The Christian music group that I am a member of, Selah, has made recording hymns a major bedrock of our music career for the past twenty-seven years. We have often used Mr. Osbeck's *101 Hymn Stories* and *101 More Hymn Stories* to research the history of the hymns we decide to record. We've always felt that doing so helped us understand the hymn better: Why was it written? Was the writer going through a difficult season of life? A beautiful season of life? What was the message the writer or writers hoped to convey through their words? We felt that knowing these things would (hopefully!) help us communicate the author's intent with an authentic, heartfelt musical performance.

I love the fact that the overall theme of this book is gratitude. In our hurried modern-day existence, it is easy to overlook the simple blessings that surround us. (I can be quite guilty of this at times, for sure!) The hymns selected for this book serve as a timeless reminder of God's tender care and love for his children. The beautiful lyrics that grace the pages of this marvelous book inspire us to pause, listen, and give thanks for the many blessings and encouragements along this journey called life.

Being a musician, I've realized that music is the best way for me to communicate my heart to someone. I tend to think of things in musical terms. To me, gratitude is like a sweet melody that, when learned and embraced, can transform our perspectives and illuminate the darkest corners of our souls. An outlook of gratitude and thanksgiving practiced in our daily lives can truly be life-changing!

As you delve into these pages, you will find each hymn transformed into a devotional experience—a moment of communion between you and our loving God. Cherish this time with him! Make use of the actionable, thought-provoking application questions in the "Living the Melody" section of each reading to help you develop and implement gratitude in your daily life.

Whether you find solace in the sanctuary of a church or the quiet corners of your heart, you can accept the invitation extended by the devotions found within these pages to embark on a spiritual journey. Each hymn, each reflection, is a stepping stone toward a deeper understanding of gratitude—a profound acknowledgment of God's divine goodness that resounds throughout the symphony of our lives.

Allan Hall of Selah

INTRODUCTION FROM THE EDITOR

I HAVE A FRIEND WHOSE life is anything but easy, yet she seems able to clamber above every single one of life's adversities—including the death of her young daughter. It isn't that she pastes on a happy face, and it isn't that she doesn't ever struggle. But she seems to have found the secret to finding her way back to a joy-filled life.

It's why I called her when my own daughter was hospitalized with a life-threatening illness. And it's her story that kept me taking steps forward after I fell backward.

Depression, anxiety, and fear may run rampant in our contemporary society, but the Bible tells us that it's possible to "take captive every thought to make it obedient to Christ" (2 Corinthians 10:5) and to choose joy (Philippians 4:4).

Scripture and science agree that we are what we think and that grateful people are joy-filled people. We can only take forward-moving steps if we orient ourselves toward truth—about our lives, our God, and our future. But where to begin?

Music is something we cannot escape. It plays in our cars, during our workouts, while we're waiting for our doctor to pick up the phone, while we're standing in an elevator. Music is everywhere. It has the power to soothe and to call to arms, to make us laugh and to make us cry . . . so why not use music to find joy by reminding ourselves of the blessings of God?

As I continue to recover from the trauma encompassing my daughter's illness, I am constantly seeking out ways to remind myself of God's goodness. That is part of why I asked to put together a book of Ken Osbeck's words on hymns of gratitude. This book is as much for me as it is for you.

In this book, you'll find updated readings from Osbeck along with a "Living the Melody" section intended to help you stand on the solid history of hymns when dealing with the mire of life.

Never forget, God is "able to do immeasurably more than all we ask or imagine, according to his power that is at work within us" (Ephesians 3:20). And we recognize his goodness with our practice of thanksgiving.

May you find God's blessings in your life today. And thanks to God's loving and powerful care, may you offer your hands in touches of that care to those around you.

Janyre Tromp

Count Your Blessings

COME THOU FOUNT

NETTLETON

ROBERT ROBINSON, 1735-1790

JOHN WYETH, 1770-1858
Arr. by Norman Johnson, 1928-

1. Come, Thou Fount of ev-'ry bless-ing, Tune my heart to sing Thy grace;
2. Here I raise mine Eb-en - e - zer— Hith-er by Thy help I'm come;
3. O to grace how great a debt-or Dai-ly I'm con-strained to be!

Streams of mer - cy, nev-er ceas-ing, Call for songs of loud-est praise.
And I hope by Thy good pleas-ure Safe-ly to ar - rive at home.
Let Thy good-ness like a fet - ter Bind my wan-d'ring heart to Thee:

Teach me some me - lo-dious son - net Sung by flam-ing tongues a - bove;
Je - sus sought me when a strang-er Wan - d'ring from the fold of God;
Prone to wan-der—Lord, I feel it— Prone to leave the God I love;

Praise the mount—I'm fixed up - on it— Mount of Thy re - deem-ing love.
He to res - cue me from dan-ger In - ter-posed His pre-cious blood.
Here's my heart— O take and seal it, Seal it for Thy courts a - bove.

— 1 —

COME, THOU FOUNT OF EVERY BLESSING

LORD, you are my God;
I will exalt you and praise your name,
for in perfect faithfulness
you have done wonderful things,
things planned long ago.
—Isaiah 25:1

ROBERT ROBINSON WAS BORN IN Norfolk, England, in 1735. His father died when Robinson was eight, and at the age of fourteen he was sent by his mother to London to learn the barbering trade. For the next few years, he associated with a notorious gang of hoodlums and led a life of debauchery.

When he was seventeen, he attended a meeting where the noted evangelist George Whitefield was preaching. Robinson went "pitying the poor, deluded Methodists; but came away envying their happiness,"[1] and ended up professing faith in Christ as his Savior. Soon Robinson felt called to preach the gospel and subsequently became the pastor of a large Baptist church in Cambridge. Despite his young age, he became known as an able minister and scholar, writing various theological books as well as several hymns, including "Come, Thou Fount of Every Blessing" when he was just twenty-three years old.

This hymn contains an interesting expression: "Here I raise mine Ebenezer—Hither by Thy help I'm come." This language is taken from 1 Samuel 7:12, where Ebenezer is a symbol of God's faithfulness: "Samuel then took a large stone and placed it between the towns of Mizpah and Jeshanah. He named it Ebenezer (which means 'the stone of help'), for he said, 'Up to this point the LORD has helped us!'" (NLT).

LIVING THE MELODY

Consider creating your own Ebenezer—a physical reminder of the ways God has helped you. Keep a thankfulness journal; create a display of memories of God's faithfulness (photos, memorabilia, words, and so on); write a series of social media posts that will pop up every year in your memories; or write good things on slips of paper, drop them into a jar, and on hard days retrieve and read one.

What Scripture Says

Just as Samuel was sacrificing the burnt offering, the Philistines arrived to attack Israel. But the LORD spoke with a mighty voice of thunder from heaven that day, and the Philistines were thrown into such confusion that the Israelites defeated them. The men of Israel chased them from Mizpah to a place below Beth-car, slaughtering them all along the way.

Samuel then took a large stone and placed it between the towns of Mizpah and Jeshanah. He named it Ebenezer (which means "the stone of help"), for he said, "Up to this point the LORD has helped us!"

—1 Samuel 7:10–12 NLT

Praise be to the Lord, to God our Savior,
    who daily bears our burdens.
—Psalm 68:19

Wisdom from History

He is everything that we find good and comforting. He is our clothing, wrapping us for love, embracing and enclosing us for tender love, so that he can never leave us, being himself everything that is good for us.[2]

—Julian of Norwich (1343–ca. 1416)

14

Julian was an English anchoress whose writings are the earliest surviving works in the English language by a woman. She survived the Black Death only to fall gravely ill at the age of thirty. During her illness she had several visions of the Lord, and after she recovered she wrote an account of them.

Application Questions

- What is a way God has provided for or helped you recently?
- How can you give praise to God for what he's done?

COUNT YOUR BLESSINGS

Johnson Oatman, Jr., 1856-1922

Edwin O. Excell, 1851-1921

1. When up-on life's bil-lows you are tem-pest-tossed, When you are dis-
2. Are you ev-er bur-dened with a load of care? Does the cross seem
3. When you look at oth-ers with their lands and gold, Think that Christ has
4. So a-mid the con-flict, wheth-er great or small, Do not be dis-

cour-aged, think-ing all is lost, Count your man-y bless-ings—name them
heav-y you are called to bear? Count your man-y bless-ings— ev-'ry
prom-ised you His wealth un-told; Count your man-y bless-ings— mon-ey
cour-aged—God is o-ver all; Count your man-y bless-ings— an-gels

one by one, And it will sur-prise you what the Lord hath done.
doubt will fly, And you will be sing-ing as the days go by.
can-not buy Your re-ward in heav-en nor your home on high.
will at-tend, Help and com-fort give you to your jour-ney's end.

CHORUS

Count your bless-ings—name them one by one; Count your
Count your man-y bless-ings— name them one by one; Count your man-y

bless-ings— see what God hath done; Count your bless-ings—
bless-ings— see what God hath done; Count your man-y bless-ings—

name them one by one; Count your man-y bless-ings—see what God hath done.

– 2 –

COUNT YOUR BLESSINGS

*Praise be to the God and Father of our Lord Jesus
Christ, who has blessed us in the heavenly realms with
every spiritual blessing in Christ.*
—Ephesians 1:3

FOR THE CHRISTIAN, GRATITUDE CAN be a life attitude.

"Count Your Blessings" was written by one of the prolific gospel
songwriters of the past century, the Methodist lay preacher Johnson J. Oatman Jr. In addition to his preaching and the writing of
more than five thousand hymn texts, Oatman was also busily engaged in a mercantile business and, in his later years, as an admini-
strator for a large insurance company in New Jersey. Other favorite
hymns by Oatman inlude "Higher Ground" and "No, Not One!"

"Count Your Blessings" is generally considered to be Oatman's
finest hymn. It has been sung all over the world. One writer stated,
"Like a beam of sunlight, it has brightened up the dark places of
earth."[3]

It is good for each of us to take time periodically to rediscover the
simple but profound truths expressed by Oatman in the four stanzas
of this hymn. In the first two stanzas, he develops the thought that
counting our blessings serves as an antidote for life's discourage-
ments and in turn makes for victorious Christian living.

The third stanza of the hymn teaches us that counting our blessings can mean that we place our material possessions in proper
perspective when compared to the eternal inheritance awaiting believers. Then, as we review our individual blessings, we certainly will
agree with Mr. Oatman's fourth stanza: the provision of God's help
and comfort to the end of our earthly pilgrimage is one of our choic-
est blessings.

Each of us could spare ourselves much despair and inner tension if we would learn to apply the practical teaching of this hymn to our daily living.

LIVING THE MELODY

Commit for the next week to begin each day by writing out three things for which you are thankful. Share them with friends and family around the dinner table, over social media, or even in a handwritten letter. When you intentionally notice your blessings, you will be surprised to see all God has done and given.

What Scripture Says
> The LORD is my strength and my shield;
>> my heart trusts in him, and he helps me.
> My heart leaps for joy,
>> and with my song I praise him.
>> —Psalm 28:7

> Every good and perfect gift is from above, coming down from the Father of the heavenly lights, who does not change like shifting shadows.
>> —James 1:17

Wisdom from History
> I have had many things in my hands, and I have lost them all; but whatever I have been able to place in God's hands, I still possess.[4]
>> —Martin Luther (1483–1546)

Luther was a German monk and theologian. He sparked the Protestant Reformation by nailing his Ninety-Five Theses to a church door, calling believers to experience the freedom found in grace through faith instead of being enslaved to religious duty.

Application Questions

- This hymn says, "When you look at others with their lands and gold, / Think that Christ has promised you his wealth untold." How does the promise of treasures in heaven change your perspective on your current situation?
- What are you thankful for in this moment?

COME, YE THANKFUL PEOPLE, COME

ST. GEORGE'S, WINDSOR

Henry Alford, 1810-1871   George J. Elvey, 1816-1893

1. Come, ye thank-ful peo-ple, come— Raise the song of har-vest-home:
2. All the world is God's own field, Fruit un-to His praise to yield:
3. For the Lord our God shall come And shall take His har-vest home:
4. E-ven so, Lord, quick-ly come To Thy fi-nal har-vest-home:

All is safe-ly gath-ered in Ere the win-ter storms be-gin.
Wheat and tares to-geth-er sown, Un-to joy or sor-row grown.
From His field shall in that day All of-fens-es purge a-way—
Gath-er Thou Thy peo-ple in, Free from sor-row, free from sin;

God, our Mak-er, doth pro-vide For our wants to be sup-plied:
First the blade and then the ear, Then the full corn shall ap-pear:
Give His an-gels charge at last In the fire the tares to cast,
There, for-ev-er pu-ri-fied, In Thy pres-ence to a-bide:

Come to God's own tem-ple, come— Raise the song of har-vest-home.
Lord of har-vest, grant that we Wholesome grain and pure may be.
But the fruit-ful ears to store In His gar-ner ev-er-more.
Come, with all Thine an-gels, come— Raise the glo-rious har-vest-home.

— 3 —

COME, YE THANKFUL PEOPLE, COME

It is good to give thanks to the LORD,
And to sing praises to Your name, O Most High.
—Psalm 92:1 NKJV

OUR EARLY AMERICAN LEADERS WISELY realized the importance of having a special day each year in which people could recount their blessings and express gratitude to God for all his goodness.

The first Thanksgiving was decreed by Governor Bradford in 1621 to commemorate the Pilgrims' harvest. Later George Washington proclaimed November 26, 1789, as a day of thanksgiving, but the holiday was not repeated on a national basis until Abraham Lincoln named it a national harvest festival on November 26, 1861. After that time the holiday was proclaimed annually by the president and the governors of each state. Finally, in 1941, Congress passed a bill naming the fourth Thursday of every November as Thanksgiving Day.

"Come, Ye Thankful People, Come" was written by Henry "Dean" Alford for the English harvest festival, a movable feast varying with the harvest time in the different villages. Alford is generally regarded as one of the most gifted Christian leaders of the nineteenth century, distinguishing himself as a theologian, scholar, writer, poet, artist, and musician.

The first stanza in "Come, Ye Thankful People, Come" invites and exhorts us to give thanks to God for his heavenly care and provision for our practical needs. The following two stanzas are an interesting commentary on the parable of the wheat and the tares as recorded in Matthew 13:24–30, 36–43. The final stanza is a prayer for the Lord's return—"Lord, quickly come to Thy final harvest-home"—the culminating event that Alford saw as the ultimate demonstration of God's goodness in his eternal purpose of man's redemption.

LIVING THE MELODY

Go to a grocery store or a farmers' market if you can. Notice the bounty, and be thankful not only for the abundance of a physical harvest but also for the spiritual bounty we have access to. Perhaps purchase a special item of produce, then steep yourself in spiritual abundance—Scripture, worship music, a gratitude-inspiring podcast, or a walk in nature with God.

What Scripture Says

Give praise to the LORD, proclaim his name;
  make known among the nations what he has done.
Sing to him, sing praise to him;
  tell of all his wonderful acts.

—1 Chronicles 16:8–9

You care for the land and water it;
  you enrich it abundantly.
The streams of God are filled with water
  to provide the people with grain,
  for so you have ordained it.
You drench its furrows and level its ridges;
  you soften it with showers and bless its crops.
You crown the year with your bounty,
  and your carts overflow with abundance.

—Psalm 65:9–11

Wisdom from History

A state of mind that sees God in everything is evidence of growth in grace and a thankful heart.[5]

—Charles Finney (1792–1875)

Finney was an American minister, leader in the Second Great Awakening, and staunch abolitionist and supporter of equal education across races and genders.

Application Questions

- Among the locally grown produce in your area, what is your favorite? Why?
- How do you see God in the food he provides?

GO TELL IT ON THE MOUNTAIN

Chorus

Go tell it on the moun-tain, O-ver the hills and ev - 'ry - where;

Fine

Go tell it on the moun-tain That Je-sus Christ is born!

1. While shep-herds kept their watch-ing O'er si-lent flocks by night,
2. The shep-herds feared and trem-bled When, lo, a-bove the earth
3. Down in a lone-ly man-ger The hum-ble Christ was born;

D. C. al Fine

Be-hold, thru-out the heav-ens There shone a ho-ly light.
Rang out the an-gel cho-rus That hailed our Sav-ior's birth.
And God sent us sal-va-tion That bless-ed Christ-mas morn.

Words: Spiritual, Vss. John W. Work, Jr (1907)
Music: Spiritual

— 4 —

GO TELL IT ON THE MOUNTAIN

You who bring good news to Zion,
go up on a high mountain.
You who bring good news to Jerusalem,
lift up your voice with a shout,
lift it up, do not be afraid;
say to the towns of Judah,
"Here is your God!"
—Isaiah 40:9

FOR MANY PEOPLE, CHRISTMAS IS merely a rerun of the trivial and the sentimental. But for the devoted Christian, Christmas is much more than that. It is a fresh awareness that a Deliverer was sent from the ivory palaces of heaven to become personally involved in the redemption and affairs of the human race. The impact of this realization becomes a strong motivation to share the good news with people who need to know that there is an Emmanuel who can meet their every need. People everywhere must hear these glad tidings if they are to benefit from them. With absolute clarity they must hear the message, "Here is your God!"

Spirituals emerged out of the late eighteenth- and early nineteenth-century camp meetings throughout the South as well as in the active evangelical ministry carried on among Black people during that time. However, few of their traditional songs were collected or published prior to about 1840.

The stanzas for "Go Tell It on the Mountain" were written by John W. Work Jr. He and his brother, Frederick J. Work, were early leaders in arranging spirituals and promoting their cause. These traditional spirituals have since become an important part of the

American folk and sacred music heritage and are greatly appreciated and enjoyed by the church at large.

LIVING THE MELODY

Knowing that the God who created the entire universe loves each of us is powerful. Gratitude and sharing our faith grow directly from a realization of the sacrifice God has made for us. Today reflect on all Jesus gave up in order to come to earth as a helpless baby.

What Scripture Says

Join in the chorus, you desert towns;
    let the villages of Kedar rejoice!
Let the people of Sela sing for joy;
    shout praises from the mountaintops!
Let the whole world glorify the LORD;
    let it sing his praise.

—Isaiah 42:11–12 NLT

My dear brothers and sisters, be strong and immovable. Always work enthusiastically for the Lord, for you know that nothing you do for the Lord is ever useless.

—1 Corinthians 15:58 NLT

Wisdom from History

We should feel with our whole heart that we have no one to rely on except God, and that from Him and Him alone can we expect every kind of good, every manner of help, and victory. Since we are nothing, we can expect nothing from ourselves, except stumblings and falls, which make us relinquish all hope of ourselves. On the other hand, we are certain always to be granted victory by God, if we arm our heart with a living trust in Him and an unshakable certainty that we will receive His help.[6]

—Lorenzo Scupoli (ca. 1530–1610)

Scupoli was unjustly accused of breaking the rules of his order and stripped of his authority and all privileges. He was completely exonerated, but not until a few years before his death. However, he did not allow the shame to stop him. He wrote a widely published practical spiritual manual for living called *The Combat*, which teaches trusting in God's power, not our own.

Application Questions

- How does reflecting on God's sacrifice affect your personal faith?
- How can you share your faith in the living Christ more effectively in the days ahead?

AMAZING GRACE

American melody
From Carrell & Clayton's *Virginia Harmony*, 1831
Arr. by Norman Johnson, 1928-

JOHN NEWTON, 1725-1807

1. A - maz - ing grace—how sweet the sound—That saved a wretch like me!
2. 'Twas grace that taught my heart to fear, And grace my fears re - lieved;
3. Thru man - y dan - gers, toils and snares I have al - read - y come;
4. When we've been there ten thou - sand years, Bright shin - ing as the sun,

I once was lost but now am found, Was blind but now I see.
How pre - cious did that grace ap - pear The hour I first be - lieved!
'Tis grace hath brought me safe thus far, And grace will lead me home.
We've no less days to sing God's praise Than when we'd first be - gun.

– 5 –

AMAZING GRACE

God is able to bless you abundantly, so that
in all things at all times . . . you will abound in
every good work.
—2 Corinthians 9:8

JOHN NEWTON, THE AUTHOR OF "Amazing Grace," left school at the age of eleven and began life as a rough, debauched seaman. Eventually he engaged in the despicable practice of capturing natives from West Africa to be sold as slaves to markets around the world. But one day the grace of God put fear into the heart of this wicked slave trader by way of a fierce storm. Fearful of a shipwreck, Newton began to read *The Imitation of Christ* by Thomas à Kempis. God used this book to lead Newton to a genuine conversion and a dramatic change in his way of life.

Newton felt convicted about his work and became a strong and effective crusader against slavery. He increasingly felt the call of God to preach the gospel and began to study diligently for the ministry. He was encouraged and greatly influenced by John and Charles Wesley and George Whitefield.

At the age of thirty-nine, Newton became an ordained minister at the Anglican church of the little village of Olney near Cambridge, England. To add further impact to his preaching, Newton incorporated simple, heartfelt hymns into his services rather than the usual psalms. When he couldn't find enough hymns, Newton wrote his own, often assisted by his close friend William Cowper. In 1779, their combined efforts produced the famous *Olney Hymns* hymnal; "Amazing Grace" is from that collection.

Until the time of his death at the age of eighty-two, John Newton never ceased to marvel at the grace of God that transformed him so completely. Shortly before his death, he is quoted as proclaiming with a loud voice during a message, "My memory is nearly gone, but I remember two things: that I am a great sinner and that Christ is a great Savior!"[7] What amazing grace!

LIVING THE MELODY

In Luke 7, a woman kneels before Jesus and cleans his feet with expensive perfume and her tears. The men around him grumble that he's allowed the woman near him. Jesus responds, "Her sins—and they are many—have been forgiven, so she has shown me much love. But a person who is forgiven little shows only little love" (v. 47 NLT). The woman, like John Newton, recognized how much Jesus had helped her, and that recognition allowed her to see and be grateful for the grace of God. Today take the time to confess where you've fallen short and thank God for his forgiveness.

What Scripture Says

Out of his fullness we have all received grace in place of grace already given. For the law was given through Moses; grace and truth came through Jesus Christ.

—John 1:16–17

The law was brought in so that the trespass might increase. But where sin increased, grace increased all the more, so that, just as sin reigned in death, so also grace might reign through righteousness to bring eternal life through Jesus Christ our Lord.

—Romans 5:20–21

Wisdom from History

God does well in giving the grace of consolation, but man does evil in not returning everything gratefully to God. Thus, the gifts of grace cannot flow in us when we are ungrateful to the Giver, when we do not return them to the

Fountainhead. Grace is always given to him who is duly grateful, and what is wont to be given the humble will be taken away from the proud.[8]

—Thomas á Kempis (ca. 1380–1471)

Á Kempis was a German-Dutch priest and author of the devotional book *The Imitation of Christ*, which emphasizes a practicable faith that leads to a real relationship with and freedom in Christ.

Application Questions

- When have you done what you wished you hadn't or did not do what you wished you had (Romans 7:15–20)?
- How can you thank God for his help, especially in the places you don't deserve it?

GLORIOUS THINGS OF THEE ARE SPOKEN

AUSTRIAN HYMN

John Newton, 1725-1807

Franz Joseph Haydn, 1732-1809

1. Glo - rious things of thee are spo - ken, Zi - on, cit - y of our God;
2. See, the streams of liv - ing wa - ters, Spring-ing from e - ter - nal love,
3. Round each hab - i - ta - tion hov-'ring, See the cloud and fire ap - pear

He whose word can - not be bro - ken Formed thee for His own a - bode:
Well sup - ply thy sons and daugh-ters And all fear of want re - move:
For a glo - ry and a cov - 'ring, Show - ing that the Lord is near!

On the Rock of A - ges found-ed, What can shake thy sure re - pose?
Who can faint while such a riv - er Ev - er flows their thirst to as-suage?
Glo - rious things of Thee are spo - ken, Zi - on, cit - y of our God;

With sal - va - tion's walls sur-round-ed, Thou mayst smile at all thy foes.
Grace which, like the Lord, the Giv - er, Nev - er fails from age to age.
He whose word can - not be bro - ken Formed thee for His own a - bode.

– 6 –

GLORIOUS THINGS OF THEE ARE SPOKEN

Great is the LORD, and greatly to be praised
In the city of our God,
In His holy mountain.
Beautiful in elevation,
The joy of the whole earth,
Is Mount Zion on the sides of the north,
The city of the great King.
God is in her palaces;
He is known as her refuge.
—Psalm 48:1–3 NKJV

OF THE MANY HYMN TEXTS written by the noted English clergyman John Newton, "Glorious Things of Thee Are Spoken" is generally considered to be one of his finest and most joyous.

In the Old Testament, the city of Zion was the place where God dwelled among his people. It was a haven of refuge, a treasured place. In our New Testament age, Zion refers to the church, a community of God's people, a living and dynamic organism. Newton's hymn refers to God's strong protection of his people, his promise to supply their needs, and his guiding presence, as with the cloud and fire for the Israelites of old.

With all its shortcomings and faults, the local body of believers is still God's means of meeting the needs of mankind. As Christians, we are to promote the church, supporting it with enthusiasm and finding our spiritual strength and fellowship in it. Then, as members of Christ's universal church, we are commanded to be his worthy representatives to the entire world. We must be actively involved in ministering the "streams of living waters" that "never fail from age to age."

John Newton, the convicted slave trader and sea captain, never stopped praising God, "whose word cannot be broken."

LIVING THE MELODY

Take time today to thank God for your community of believers and what they mean in your life. Thank him for fulfilling his promises and providing the church as a place of refuge. Ask for God's special blessing on your leaders, on the Christians who influence you, and on those who walk beside you. If you don't currently have a place of refuge, consider becoming active in a local church body.

What Scripture Says

Look on Zion, the city of our festivals;
>   your eyes will see Jerusalem,
>   a peaceful abode, a tent that will not be moved;
its stakes will never be pulled up,
>   nor any of its ropes broken.
There the LORD will be our Mighty One.
>   It will be like a place of broad rivers and streams.
No galley with oars will ride them,
>   no mighty ship will sail them.

—Isaiah 33:20–21

By this everyone will know that you are my disciples, if you love one another.

—John 13:35

Wisdom from History

Our life and our death are with our neighbour. If we gain our brother, we have gained God; but if we scandalize our brother, we have sinned against Christ.[9]

—Anthony the Great (251–356)

Anthony was a Christian monk from Egypt known as the "Father of Monks." As one of the first to sojourn into the desert wilderness alone, Anthony was quite famous, a status that was reinforced when his biography, *The Life of Anthony*, was written and disseminated by Athanasius of Alexandria.

Application Questions

- Where is your Zion (place of refuge on earth)?
- How has God used your church or the church in your area to minister to you?

HIS LOVING-KINDNESS

1. A - wake, my soul, to joy - ful lays, And sing thy great
2. He saw me ru - ined by the fall, Yet loved me, not
3. Tho' nu - m'rous hosts of might - y foes, Tho' earth and hell
4. When trou - ble, like a gloom - y cloud, Has gath - ered thick

Re - deem - er's praise; He just - ly claims a song for me:
with - stand - ing all; He saved me from my lost es - tate:
my way op - pose, He safe - ly leads my soul a - long:
and thun - dered loud, He near my soul has al - ways stood:

His lov - ing - kind - ness, O how free! Lov - ing - kind - ness,
His lov - ing - kind - ness, O how great! Lov - ing - kind - ness,
His lov - ing - kind - ness, O how strong! Lov - ing - kind - ness,
His lov - ing - kind - ness, O how good! Lov - ing - kind - ness,

Lov - ing - kind - ness, His lov - ing - kind - ness, O how free!
Lov - ing - kind - ness, His lov - ing - kind - ness, O how great!
Lov - ing - kind - ness, His lov - ing - kind - ness, O how strong!
Lov - ing - kind - ness, His lov - ing - kind - ness, O how good!

Words: Samuel Medley
Music: William Caldwell

– 7 –

HIS LOVING-KINDNESS

How priceless is your unfailing love, O God!
People take refuge in the shadow of your wings.
—Psalm 36:7

LOVING-KINDNESS HAS BEEN DESCRIBED as love in action. Because of God's loving-kindness in the act of sending Christ to be our Redeemer while we were still sinners (Romans 5:8), Christians have a reason for singing about the Lord. "His praise will always be on my lips" (Psalm 34:1).

The author of "His Loving-Kindness," Samuel Medley, lived a self-indulgent life in the British Navy until he was severely wounded in a sea fight between the French and English in 1759, off Cape Lagos, Portugal.

While convalescing, Medley read a sermon by Isaac Watts on Isaiah 42:6–7, which says, "I, the LORD, have called you in righteousness; I will take hold of your hand. I will . . . release from the dungeon those who sit in darkness." These verses ultimately led to Medley's conversion and later to his becoming a minister of the gospel.

For twenty-seven years Medley pastored the Baptist church in Liverpool with much success, especially as a preacher to the sailors. Medley wrote a large number of hymns but always stated in the preface of his hymnbooks that his only purpose for writing was to "encourage and comfort the hearts of true christians [*sic*] . . . to glorify my great God and Redeemer."[10] It has been said that the underlying purpose of Samuel Medley's ministry, both in preaching and in hymn writing, was "to humble the pride of man, exalt the grace of God in his own salvation, and promote real holiness in heart and life."[11]

First published in 1782, "His Loving-Kindness" was written as

Medley's personal testimony of thanksgiving to God for his free and great loving-kindness.

LIVING THE MELODY

Think back to when you first encountered God. Write out your salvation experience. Reflect on God's leading and anticipate the eternal joys of heaven. Then sing or hum as you go about the rest of your day.

What Scripture Says

"Though the mountains be shaken
 and the hills be removed,
yet my unfailing love for you will not be shaken
 nor my covenant of peace be removed,"
 says the LORD, who has compassion on you.
—Isaiah 54:10

Because of his great love for us, God, who is rich in mercy, made us alive with Christ even when we were dead in transgressions—it is by grace you have been saved. And God raised us up with Christ and seated us with him in the heavenly realms in Christ Jesus, in order that in the coming ages he might show the incomparable riches of his grace, expressed in his kindness to us in Christ Jesus.
—Ephesians 2:4–7

Wisdom from History

Looking with purest gaze at the rewards promised to the saints, our spirit is moved by measureless joy to pour out wordless thanksgiving to God.[12]
—Saint John Cassian (360–435)

Saint John Cassian was born in the modern-day area of Romania and Bulgaria. His writings were a major influence on the establishment of monastic institutions and ideas in medieval Western culture.

Application Questions

- How have you seen God's loving-kindness play out in your life?
- What are some of the "rewards promised to the saints" that you are most grateful for right now?

I LOVE TO TELL THE STORY

A. CATHERINE HANKEY, 1834-1911

WILLIAM G. FISCHER, 1835-1912

1. I love to tell the story Of un-seen things a-bove, Of
Je - sus and His glo-ry, Of Je - sus and His love; I love to
tell the sto-ry Be-cause I know 'tis true, It sat-is-fies my
long-ings As noth-ing else can do.

2. I love to tell the story— More won-der-ful it seems Than
all the gold-en fan-cies Of all our gold-en dreams; I love to
tell the sto-ry— It did so much for me, And that is just the
rea - son I tell it now to thee.

3. I love to tell the story— 'Tis pleas-ant to re-peat What
seems, each time I tell it, More won-der-ful-ly sweet; I love to
tell the sto-ry For some have nev-er heard The mes-sage of sal-
va - tion From God's own ho - ly Word.

4. I love to tell the story, For those who know it best Seem
hun-ger-ing and thirst-ing To hear it like the rest; And when in
scenes of glo-ry I sing the new, new song, 'Twill be the old, old
sto - ry That I have loved so long.

REFRAIN

I love to tell the sto-ry! 'Twill be my theme in glo-ry— To tell the old, old sto-ry Of Je-sus and His love.

– 8 –

I LOVE TO TELL THE STORY

The fruit of the righteous is a tree of life,
And he who wins souls is wise.
—Proverbs 11:30 NKJV

SHARING OUR PERSONAL FAITH WITH others can be a joyful and satisfying experience, a product of our commitment to discipleship and our daily, intimate relationship with the Lord. It isn't salesmanship or an attempt to manipulate individuals to a decision. It is simply taking a message—the objective historical truths of the gospel—and then speaking with the authority of Jesus Christ in the power and love of the Holy Spirit.

A. Catherine Hankey, author of "I Love to Tell the Story," was born in 1834 into the home of a wealthy English banker. Her family were prominent members of the Anglican church, and they were involved in an evangelistic movement in England. Early in her life, Hankey developed this same concern for evangelism. She began organizing Sunday school classes for rich and poor throughout London. These classes had a strong influence in the city, with a large number of the young students in turn becoming zealous Christian workers.

When Hankey was only thirty years old, she experienced a serious illness. During the long period of recovery, she wrote a lengthy poem on the life of Christ. The poem consisted of two main sections, each containing fifty verses. The first section of the poem, titled "The Story Wanted," was later adapted for another of Hankey's familiar hymn texts, "Tell Me the Old, Old Story," and is still widely sung today. Later that same year, while recovering from her illness, Hankey completed the second part of her poem, titled "The Story Told," which became the main portion of "I Love to Tell the Story."

LIVING THE MELODY

Jesus often said he came to help those who were suffering rather than those who felt they had life in hand (see Matthew 9:12–13). If we approach proclaiming the good news similarly, we will act as one contented beggar telling a starving beggar friend where there is food. Today identify one way God has shown up for you, and look for ways to tell others about God's love for them.

What Scripture Says

In your hearts revere Christ as Lord. Always be prepared to give an answer to everyone who asks you to give the reason for the hope that you have. But do this with gentleness and respect.

—1 Peter 3:15

This is how God showed his love among us: He sent his one and only Son into the world that we might live through him. This is love: not that we loved God, but that he loved us and sent his Son as an atoning sacrifice for our sins.

—1 John 4:9–10

Wisdom from History

When you sit down to eat, pray. When you eat bread, do so thanking Him for being so generous to you. If you drink wine, be mindful of Him who has given it to you for your pleasure and as a relief in sickness. When you dress, thank Him for His kindness in providing you with clothes. When you look at the sky and the beauty of the stars, throw yourself at God's feet and adore Him who in His wisdom has arranged things in this way. Similarly, when the sun goes down and when it rises, when you are asleep or awake, give thanks to God, who created and arranged all things for your benefit, to have you know, love and praise their Creator.[13]

—Saint Basil of Caesarea (330–379)

Saint Basil was a bishop in Asia Minor (modern-day Turkey) known for the way he cared for the poor and emphasized that all people are equal in the sight of God.

Application Questions

- Is it easier to see God working when times are easy or difficult? Why?
- What is a story you can tell others about how Jesus has come through for you?

I WILL PRAISE HIM!

Margaret Jenkins Harris, 1898

Margaret Jenkins Harris

1. When I saw the cleans-ing fount-ain O-pen wide for all my sin,
2. Though the way seems straight and nar-row, All I claimed was swept a - way;
3. Then God's fire up - on the al - tar Of my heart was set a - flame;
4. Bless - èd be the name of Je - sus! I'm so glad He took me in;
5. Glo - ry, glo - ry to the Fa - ther! Glo-ry, glo - ry to the Son!

I o - beyed the Spir - it's woo - ing, When He said, "Wilt thou be clean?"
My am - bi - tions, plans and wish - es, At my feet in ash - es lay.
I shall ne - ver cease to praise Him Glo - ry, glo - ry to His name!
He's for - giv - en my trans - gress - ions, He has cleansed my heart from sin.
Glo - ry, glo - ry to the Spir - it! Glo - ry to the Three in One!

Refrain

I will praise Him! I will praise Him! Praise the Lamb for sin-ners slain;

Give Him glo-ry, all ye peo-ple, For His blood can wash a - way each stain.

— 9 —

I WILL PRAISE HIM!

To him who loves us and has freed us from our sins
by his blood, and has made us to be a kingdom and
priests to serve his God and Father—to him be glory
and power for ever and ever! Amen.
—Revelation 1:5–6

AN ATTITUDE OF HAPPINESS IN life is a matter of our will. It is thought to have been Abraham Lincoln who once stated that "most people are as happy as they make up their minds to be."

Closely related to a Christian's happiness is the determination to live a life of praise to God. The goal of every believer should be to overflow with praise regardless of the circumstances. Knowing God in Christ is the most compelling reason to have such a life. Each day is a new opportunity to offer a praise sacrifice to God. Instead of dwelling on the negatives of our lives, we can seek fresh reasons daily for praising our Lord.

Praise is our highest spiritual exercise. There is more said in the Scriptures about our praise life than even our times of prayer. In prayer it is possible to approach God out of selfish motives; in praise, we worship him for what he is himself. Praise is also an encouragement to others: "I will glory in the LORD; let the afflicted hear and rejoice" (Psalm 34:2). Weak hearts will be strengthened and trembling saints revived when they hear our testimonies of praise.

One of the most important times to sing praise to God is when we feel imprisoned by the circumstances of life. Like the experience of Paul and Silas in the Roman prison (Acts 16:24–26), it is often uncanny how prayer and praise open the doors of our lives to new dimensions of opportunity and spiritual power.

LIVING THE MELODY

Margaret Jenkins Harris, the author of "I Will Praise Him!," and her husband were active musicians and song evangelists in the American Midwest during the early twentieth century. The couple lived a life dedicated to praising God and brought that worship and encouragement to thousands. What a benchmark to aim for!

When we determine to live a life of praise, we are able to take every thought captive. Begin by noticing when your thoughts veer toward the negative. Then purposefully turn toward gratitude. You may even consider making a list of fresh reasons to rejoice and sing praise to God.

What Scripture Says

I will extol the LORD at all times;
　　his praise will always be on my lips.
I will glory in the LORD;
　　let the afflicted hear and rejoice.
Glorify the LORD with me;
　　let us exalt his name together.
　　　　　　　　　　—Psalm 34:1–3

Oh, the depth of the riches of the wisdom and knowledge of God! . . .
For from him and through him and for him are all things.
　　To him be the glory forever! Amen.
　　　　　　　　　　—Romans 11:33, 36

Wisdom from History

When we lose one blessing, another is often most unexpectedly given in its place.[14]
　　　　　　　　　　—C. S. Lewis (1898–1963)

Lewis was an author, apologist, scholar, and theologian. He taught at Oxford and Cambridge, and was a prolific writer of fiction and nonfiction. Some of his most famous works include *Mere Christianity*, *The Screwtape Letters*, and the Chronicles of Narnia.

Application Questions

- What negative thought has become a pattern in your life?
- What aspect of God's goodness have you experienced that you can praise him for?
- How is praise sometimes a sacrifice?

IN MY HEART THERE RINGS A MELODY

Elton M. Roth, 1891-1951   Elton M. Roth, 1891-1951

1. I have a song that Je-sus gave me, It was sent from
2. I love the Christ who died on Cal-v'ry, For He washed my
3. 'Twill be my end-less theme in glo-ry, With the an-gels

heav'n a-bove; There nev-er was a sweet-er mel-o-dy, 'Tis a
sins a-way; He put with-in my heart a mel-o-dy, And I
I will sing; 'Twill be a song with glo-rious har-mo-ny, When the

mel-o-dy of love.
know it's there to stay.   In my heart there rings a mel-o-dy,
courts of heav-en ring.

CHORUS

There rings a mel-o-dy with heav-en's har-mo-ny;   In my

heart there rings a mel-o-dy; There rings a mel-o-dy of love.

IN MY HEART THERE RINGS A MELODY

Sing to the LORD a new song,
for he has done marvelous things;
his right hand and his holy arm
have worked salvation for him. . . .
Shout for joy to the LORD, all the earth,
burst into jubilant song with music.
—Psalm 98:1, 4

KING SOLOMON, ONE OF THE wisest men who ever lived, once observed, "A happy heart makes the face cheerful, but heartache crushes the spirit" (Proverbs 15:13). Those in the medical profession have long realized that happy people are the healthiest people. But how does one achieve that happiness, that joy? The child of God knows that it comes from living close to the Savior. And joy experienced can also be joy expressed.

This can be true in our individual lives as well as when we gather in our church services. True worship must have the ingredient of festal joy. The Psalms insist that we "burst into jubilant song with music" (98:4) and that we praise our God with trumpet, lute, harp, timbrel, and loud crashing cymbals. Too often believers give the impression that the Christian experience is a cheerless journey of harsh self-discipline that must be painfully endured until the heavenly rewards are finally realized. There is little joy or praise in such a testimony.

The author and composer of "In My Heart There Rings a Melody," Elton M. Roth, was a well-known musician of his day. While assisting with evangelistic meetings in Texas on a hot summer day in 1923, the words and music for this hymn suddenly came to him. Roth recalled, "That evening I introduced the song by having more than two hundred boys and girls sing it at the open air meeting, after which the audience joined in the singing. I was thrilled as it seemed my whole being was transformed into song."

When our worship and personal experience are full of joy and song, we live in such a way that encourages others to know this same happiness.

LIVING THE MELODY

Consider these questions: Am I truly a happy Christian? Does my life express the joy of the Lord? Does my church worship produce joy in my life?

Ask God to change whatever may be lacking, and consider creating an event dedicated to celebration. Invite fellow believers, neighbors, or whomever you have connections with. Sing, read poetry, paint, or simply walk in nature to notice the amazing things God has created.

What Scripture Says

Give praise to the LORD, proclaim his name;
>   make known among the nations what he has done.
Sing to him, sing praise to him;
>   tell of all his wonderful acts.
Glory in his holy name;
>   let the hearts of those who seek the LORD rejoice.
>   —1 Chronicles 16:8–10

Nehemiah said, "Go and enjoy choice food and sweet drinks, and send some to those who have nothing prepared. This day is holy to our Lord. Do not grieve, for the joy of the LORD is your strength."

>   —Nehemiah 8:10

Wisdom from History

Thanks are the highest form of thought, and . . . gratitude is happiness doubled by wonder.[15]
>   —G. K. Chesterton (1874–1936)

Chesterton was an English social and literature critic, essayist, and fiction writer, perhaps best known for his fictional character Father Brown. But he was also a devout believer and apologist whose insight is appreciated to this day.

Application Questions

- Where do you see scriptural evidence that celebration is important for one's spiritual life?
- What can you celebrate today?

IN THE CROSS OF CHRIST I GLORY

RATHBUN

JOHN BOWRING, 1792-1872

ITHAMAR CONKEY, 1815-1867

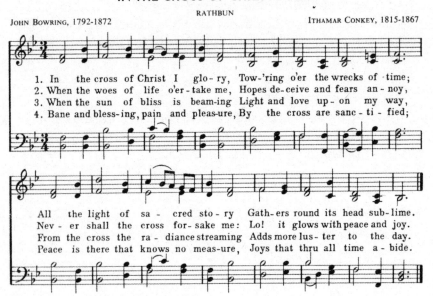

1. In the cross of Christ I glo-ry, Tow-'ring o'er the wrecks of time;
2. When the woes of life o'er-take me, Hopes de-ceive and fears an-noy,
3. When the sun of bliss is beam-ing Light and love up-on my way,
4. Bane and bless-ing, pain and pleas-ure, By the cross are sanc-ti-fied;

All the light of sa-cred sto-ry Gath-ers round its head sub-lime.
Nev-er shall the cross for-sake me: Lo! it glows with peace and joy.
From the cross the ra-diance streaming Adds more lus-ter to the day.
Peace is there that knows no meas-ure, Joys that thru all time a-bide.

IN THE CROSS OF CHRIST I GLORY

*May I never boast except in the cross of our Lord Jesus
Christ, through which the world has been crucified to
me, and I to the world.*
—Galatians 6:14

THE CROSS HAS BEEN THE most significant symbol of the Christian faith throughout church history. As many as four hundred different forms or designs of it have been used—among them the usual Latin cross, Greek cross, and budded cross. Regardless of design, the symbol of the cross should always remind us of the price that was paid by the eternal God for humanity's redemption.

"In the Cross of Christ I Glory" is generally considered one of the finest hymns about the cross. It was written by John Bowring, one of the most remarkable men of his day and one of the greatest linguists who ever lived. It is said that he could converse in over one hundred languages.

Some writers claim Bowring had visited Macao on the southern China coast and been much impressed by the sight of a bronze cross towering on the summit of a massive wall of what had once been a great cathedral. Built by early Portuguese colonists, the cathedral had overlooked the harbor and been destroyed by a typhoon. Only the one wall, topped by the huge metal cross, remained. This scene is said to have so impressed Bowring that it eventually served as the inspiration for his hymn text.

The tune for this hymn was composed by Ithamar Conkey, an American organist and choir leader of the Central Baptist Church of Norwich, Connecticut, twenty-four years after the original text was written.

Conkey was sorely disappointed at a Sunday morning service when only one choir member appeared, a faithful soprano by the name of Mrs. Beriah Rathbun. Before the evening service, Conkey composed a new tune for this text and named it "Rathbun."

The preaching of the cross may sound foolish to many, "but to us who are being saved it is the power of God" (1 Corinthians 1:18).

LIVING THE MELODY

Christ's death and resurrection are the cornerstone of our faith because his redeeming sacrifice has set us in right relationship with God. In celebration of this truth, consider purchasing or creating a cross. Then put it where you see it often so it can be a visible reminder of what Christ has done for you and of your status as a free child of God.

What Scripture Says

Have the same mindset as Christ Jesus:

Who, being in very nature God,
    did not consider equality with God something to be used
to his own advantage;
rather, he made himself nothing
    by taking the very nature of a servant,
    being made in human likeness.
And being found in appearance as a man,
    he humbled himself
    by becoming obedient to death—
        even death on a cross!

Therefore God exalted him to the highest place
    and gave him the name that is above every name,
    . . . to the glory of God the Father.
—Philippians 2:5–9, 11

Wisdom from History

When we are speaking about truth and life and redemption, we are speaking about Christ.[16]

—Saint Ambrose (339–397)

Saint Ambrose was a wealthy governor when he was unexpectedly given the position of bishop of Milan in order to prevent conflict in the region. With his preaching, innovations in hymnography, asceticism, and fierce protection of the faith, Ambrose quickly became one of the most influential clerics of early Christianity.

Application Questions

- What does the cross mean to you?
- What are some other symbols of God's blessings in your life?

MY FAITH HAS FOUND A RESTING PLACE

1. My faith has found a rest-ing place, Not in a man-made creed;
2. E-nough for me that Je-sus saves, This ends my fear and doubt;
3. My soul is rest-ing on the Word, The liv-ing Word of God:
4. The great Phy-si-cian heals the sick, The lost He came to save;

I trust the ev-er liv-ing One, That He for me will plead.
A sin-ful soul I come to Him, He will not cast me out.
Sal-va-tion by my Sav-ior's name, Sal-va-tion through His blood.
For me His pre-cious blood He shed, For me His life He gave.

Chorus

I need no oth-er ar-gu-ment, I need no oth-er plea;

It is e-nough that Je-sus died And rose a-gain for me.

Words: Lidie H. Edmunds
Music: Norwegian Melody, Arr. by William J. Kirkpatrick

— 12 —

MY FAITH HAS FOUND A RESTING PLACE

*I know whom I have believed, and am convinced
that he is able to guard what I have entrusted to him
until that day.*
—2 Timothy 1:12

SAVING FAITH IS MUCH MORE than a commitment to a creed, church, or doctrinal system. It's a committment to a person—Jesus Christ. While doctrinal statements and creeds are important in defining and delineating truth, they must never replace a personal relationship with the Truth.

We can get so caught up in our creedal statements, interpretations and arguments, or church traditions that we lose the sense of simple, childlike trust in Christ and his written Word. This was the concern of the apostle Paul—"I am afraid that just as Eve was deceived by the serpent's cunning, your minds may somehow be led astray from your sincere and pure devotion to Christ" (2 Corinthians 11:3).

Again and again we must take inventory of ourselves to determine what is the real foundation of our spiritual lives and the source of our resting place—Christ or merely a creed.

Little is known about either Lidie H. Edmunds, the author of the text for "My Faith Has Found a Resting Place," or the source of the tune, other than that it is an old Norwegian melody.

The hymn in its present form first appeared in the hymnal *Songs of Joy and Gladness*, published in 1891. It has become increasingly popular in recent years as a testimonial hymn in church services. May it testify of your faith in God.

LIVING THE MELODY

It is tempting to place our faith on certain doctrines, traditions, or rules. Checking a list of dos and don'ts might feel safer and less vulnerable at times, but maintaining a performance-based righteousness is a heavy load to carry. Christ invites us to rest in him alone: "Come to me, all you who are weary and burdened, and I will give you rest. Take my yoke upon you and learn from me, for I am gentle and humble in heart, and you will find rest for your souls" (Matthew 11:28–29).

Meditate on the words of this hymn today, and give thanks to God that you can rest in him because he has redeemed you.

What Scripture Says

But as for me, I know that my Redeemer lives,
   and he will stand upon the earth at last.
And after my body has decayed,
   yet in my body I will see God!
I will see him for myself.
   Yes, I will see him with my own eyes.
   I am overwhelmed at the thought!
                    —Job 19:25–27 NLT

And this is what God has testified: He has given us eternal life, and this life is in his Son. Whoever has the Son has life; whoever does not have God's Son does not have life.

I have written this to you who believe in the name of the Son of God, so that you may know you have eternal life.
                    —1 John 5:11–13 NLT

Wisdom from History

Joy is the simplest form of gratitude.[17]
                    —Karl Barth (1886–1968)

Barth was a Protestant theologian from Switzerland. He was the main author of "The Barmen Declaration," a document that countered the Nazi ideology that had infiltrated the church. This declaration was adopted by the German Confessing Church, a group opposed to the Third Reich.

Application Questions

- How is learning the creeds different from building a relationship with Christ? (If you're unfamiliar with the creeds, look up the text of the Apostles' Creed.)
- Take inventory of yourself, as Osbeck encourages. In practice, what is the foundation of your faith?

NOW THANK WE ALL OUR GOD

NUN DANKET

Martin Rinkart, 1586-1649
Trans. by Catherine Winkworth, 1827-1878

Johann Crüger, 1598-1662
Arr. by Eldon Burkwall, 1928-

1. Now thank we all our God With hearts and hands and voic - es,
2. O may this boun-teous God Thru all our life be near us,
3. All praise and thanks to God The Fa - ther now be giv - en,

Who won-drous things hath done, In whom His world re - joic - es;
With ev - er joy - ful hearts And bless-ed peace to cheer us;
The Son and Him who reigns With Them in high-est heav - en—

Who from our moth-ers' arms Hath blessed us on our way
And keep us in His grace, And guide us when per - plexed,
The one e - ter - nal God Whom earth and heav'n a - dore—

With count-less gifts of love, And still is ours to - day.
And free us from all ills In this world and the next.
For thus it was, is now, And shall be ev - er - more.

NOW THANK WE ALL OUR GOD

Who shall separate us from the love of Christ? Shall
trouble or hardship or persecution or famine
or nakedness or danger or sword? . . . No, in all
these things we are more than conquerors
through him who loved us.
—Romans 8:35, 37

SOME OF THE SEVEREST HUMAN suffering imaginable occurred during the Thirty Years' War (1618–48). Yet from this war that has been described as the most devastating in all history, the great hymn "Now Thank We All Our God" was born.

Martin Rinkart was called at the age of thirty-one to pastor the state Lutheran church in his native city of Eilenburg, Germany. He arrived there just as the dreadful bloodshed of the Thirty Years' War began, and there Rinkart spent the remaining thirty-two years of his life faithfully ministering to his needy people.

Germany, the battleground of the conflict between warring Catholic and Protestant forces from various countries throughout Europe, was reduced to a state of misery that baffles description. The German population dwindled from sixteen million to six million. Because Eilenburg was a walled city, it became a frightfully overcrowded refuge for political and military fugitives from far and near. Throughout these war years, several waves of deadly diseases and famines swept the city as the various armies marched through the town, leaving death and destruction in their wake.

The plague of 1637 was particularly severe. At its height, Rinkart was the only minister remaining to care for the sick and dying. His triumphant, personal expressions of gratitude and confidence in God confirm the truth taught in Scripture: we, as God's children, can be "more than conquerors through him who loved us" (Romans 8:37).

LIVING THE MELODY

Scripture is clear that we will all experience difficulty (James 1:2). But God has equipped us to be victors, not victims, of life. Rinkart's hymn offers a key to thankfulness even amid troublesome times: "O may this bounteous God / Thru all our life be near us."

With God's presence we can overcome and not be overwhelmed. It's a matter of trusting that our all-powerful God cares enough that "in all things [he] works for the good of those who love him" (Romans 8:28). Next time you feel overwhelmed by circumstance, notice the anxiety, acknowledge it, and bring it to God, trusting that he loves you and will not leave you (Hebrews 13:5).

What Scripture Says

Blessed be the LORD God of Israel
From everlasting to everlasting!
—1 Chronicles 16:36 NKJV

But thank God! He gives us victory over sin and death through our Lord Jesus Christ.

So, my dear brothers and sisters, be strong and immovable. Always work enthusiastically for the Lord, for you know that nothing you do for the Lord is ever useless.
—1 Corinthians 15:57–58 NLT

Wisdom from History

A brother asked Abba Poemen, "How should a man behave?" The old man said to him, "Look at Daniel: no-one found anything in him to complain about except for his prayers to the Lord his God."[18]
—Poemen the Great (ca. 340–450)

Poemen was a Desert Father who lived at a monastery in Scetis (or Skete), now the Wadi El Natrun. During his time there, the monastery was attacked by raiders, causing the monks to scatter. He and the other monks with him are responsible for preserving the wise sayings of the Desert Fathers.

Application Questions

- What is making you feel anxious today? How can you bring your anxiety to God?
- How have your expectations about whether life would be easy or hard affected the way you relate to God?

PRAISE HIM! PRAISE HIM!

1. Praise Him! Praise Him! Je-sus, our bless-ed Re-deem-er! Sing, O Earth, His
2. Praise Him! Praise Him! Je-sus, our bless-ed Re-deem-er! For our sins He
3. Praise Him! Praise Him! Je-sus, our bless-ed Re-deem-er! Heav'n-ly por-tals

won-der-ful love pro-claim! Hail Him! Hail Him! High-est arch-an-gels in
suf-fered, and bled, and died. He our Rock, our hope of e-ter-nal sal-
loud with hos-an-nas ring! Je-sus, Sav-ior, liv-eth for-ev-er and

D.S.– Praise Him! Praise Him! tell of His ex-cel-lent

Fine

glo-ry; Strength and hon-or give to His ho-ly Name! Like a shep-herd,
va-tion; Hail Him! Hail Him! Je-sus the Cru-ci-fied. Sound His prais-es!
ev-er. Crown Him! Crown Him! Proph-et, and Priest, and King! Christ is com-ing!

great-ness; Praise Him! Praise Him! ev-er in joy-ful song!

D.S. al Fine

Je-sus will guard His child-ren, In His arms He car-ries them all day long;
Je-sus who bore our sor-rows, Love un-bound-ed, won-der-ful, deep and strong;
O-ver the world vic-to-rious, Pow'r and glo-ry un-to the Lord be-long;

Words by Fanny J. Crosby
Music by Chester G. Allen

– 14 –

PRAISE HIM! PRAISE HIM!

I will praise the LORD all my life;
I will sing praise to my God as long as I live.
—Psalm 146:2

PRAISE IS OUR LORD'S MOST righteous due. Scriptures clearly teach that we are to offer a sacrifice of praise to God continually (Hebrews 13:15–16). Offering praise is not an option—it is one of God's commands.

Our daily sacrifice of praise includes joyful songs for who Christ is—"our blessed Redeemer." We also praise God for all his daily blessings, which are beyond number. We can even offer praise for the trials of life, for they are often blessings in disguise. Finally, our sacrifice includes praise for his leading in ways yet to be experienced.

"Praise Him! Praise Him!" is one of the many favorite gospel hymns written by Fanny J. Crosby, an American poet. Crosby lost her sight at six weeks of age because of improper medical treatment. However, she considered her blindness a blessing.

At one time a well-intentioned minister remarked to her, "I think it is a great pity that the good Master, when he showered so many gifts upon you, did not give you sight." Fanny replied, "If at my birth I had been able to have made one petition to my Creator, it would have been that I should be made blind." The suprised clergyman asked her why, and she responded, "Because, when I get to heaven, the first face that shall ever gladden my sight will be that of my Saviour!"[19]

In all, Crosby wrote between eight thousand and nine thousand gospel hymn texts, supplying our hymnals with more beloved songs than any other hymn writer.

"Praise Him! Praise Him!" first appeared in *Bright Jewels for the Sunday School*, which was published in 1869. The song was originally titled "Praise, Give Thanks." Still today, these words evoke praise from each believing heart.

LIVING THE MELODY

Though we're commanded to praise God, he doesn't want our praise to come from a place of obligation. A key to authentic praise is our focus. Do we focus on the delays, frustrations, losses, and pain? Or do we see opportunities in the waiting, bounty in our frustration, blessings inside the loss, and faith in our pain? It's a matter of choice.

Today go forth with a renewed awareness of Christ's presence in your life, and offer him this sacrifice of praise.

What Scripture Says

I looked again, and I heard the voices of thousands and millions of angels around the throne and of the living beings and the elders. And they sang in a mighty chorus:

"Worthy is the Lamb who was slaughtered—
    to receive power and riches
and wisdom and strength
    and honor and glory and blessing."

And then I heard every creature in heaven and on earth and under the earth and in the sea. They sang:

"Blessing and honor and glory and power
    belong to the one sitting on the throne
    and to the Lamb forever and ever."

And the four living beings said, "Amen!" And the twenty-four elders fell down and worshiped the Lamb.

—Revelation 5:11–14 NLT

Wisdom from History

Christianity is not a theory, or a speculation; but a life;—not a philosophy of life, but a life and a living process.[20]

—Samuel Taylor Coleridge (1772–1834)

Coleridge was an English poet, philosopher, theologian, and critic who was a cofounder of the Romantic movement. Though he grew up attending a charity school and never graduated college, he was an immensely deep thinker and is widely acknowledged as one of the most important English poets.

Application Questions

- In what ways have you seen God's goodness today?
- What is a burden that turned out to be a blessing in your life?

PRAISE TO THE LORD, THE ALMIGHTY

1. Praise to the Lord, the Al-might-y, the King of cre-a-tion! O my soul, praise Him, for He is thy health and sal-va-tion! All ye who hear, now to His tem-ple draw near; Join me in glad ad-o-ra-tion!

2. Praise to the Lord, Who o'er all things so won-drous-ly reign-eth, Shel-ters thee un-der His wings, yea, so gen-tly sus-tain-eth! Hast thou not seen how thy de-sires e'er have been Grant-ed in what He or-dain-eth?

3. Praise to the Lord, Who doth pros-per thy work and de-fend thee, Sure-ly His good-ness and mer-cy here dai-ly at-tend thee. Pon-der a-new what the Al-might-y can do, If with His love He be-friend thee.

4. Praise to the Lord! O let all that is in me a-dore Him! All that hath life and breath, come now with prais-es be-fore Him! Let the a-men sound from His peo-ple a-gain; Glad-ly for ev-er a-dore Him.

Words: Joachim Neander
Music: Erneuerten Gesangbuch, Stralsund

– 15 –

PRAISE TO THE LORD, THE ALMIGHTY

May the peoples praise you, God;
may all the peoples praise you.
—Psalm 67:3

GREAT EXPRESSIONS OF PRAISE TO God have come from many different traditions and backgrounds. Throughout the centuries God has used the talents of people from various cultures to provide his church with hymns of worship.

The author of this inspiring hymn text, Joachim Neander, has often been called the greatest of all German Calvinist hymn writers. He wrote approximately sixty hymns and composed many tunes. Nearly all his hymns are triumphant expressions of praise. Neander, though only thirty years of age when he died, was a noted scholar in theology, literature, and music, as well as the pastor of the Reformed Church in Düsseldorf, Germany.

"Praise to the Lord, the Almighty" is a free paraphrase of Psalm 103:1–6, which begins, "Bless [praise] the LORD, O my soul; And all that is within me, bless His holy name" (NKJV).

The translator of this text, Catherine Winkworth, is regarded as one of the finest translators of the German language. Her translations helped make German hymns popular in England and America during the nineteenth century. The tune, *Lobe Den Herren* ("Praise to the Lord"), first appeared in a German hymnal in 1665. It is said that Neander personally chose this tune for his text, and the words have never been used with any other melody.

LIVING THE MELODY

As the king of creation, God wields power over all things, giving "his sunlight to both the evil and the good, and [sending] rain on the just and the unjust alike" (Matthew 5:45 NLT). As a result, "the mountains and hills will burst into song, and the trees of the field will clap their hands!" (Isaiah 55:12 NLT). What a beautiful picture of creation coming alongside us to give praise to our almighty Creator.

Today notice how all of creation points to God, and join creation in praising him with your entire being—heart, soul, and mind.

What Scripture Says

Let all that I am praise the LORD;
with my whole heart, I will praise his holy name.
Let all that I am praise the LORD;
may I never forget the good things he does for me.
He forgives all my sins
and heals all my diseases.
He redeems me from death
and crowns me with love and tender mercies.
He fills my life with good things.
My youth is renewed like the eagle's!

The LORD gives righteousness
and justice to all who are treated unfairly.
—Psalm 103:1–6 NLT

O LORD, what a variety of things you have made!
In wisdom you have made them all.
The earth is full of your creatures.
—Psalm 104:24 NLT

Wisdom from History

There are two books laid before us to study, to prevent our falling into error; first, the volume of the Scriptures, which reveal the will of God; then the volume of the Creatures, which express His power.[21]

—Francis Bacon (1561–1626)

Bacon was a devout Christian, scientist, and philosopher most well-known for his development of an empirical method of scientific observation known as the Baconian method.

Application Questions

- What would it feel like for you to praise God with your whole being—heart, soul, and mind?
- What part of creation causes you to give God thanks?

REJOICE—THE LORD IS KING!

1. Re - joice, the Lord is King; Your Lord and King a - dore!
2. Je - sus, the Sav - ior, reigns, The God of truth and love;
3. Re - joice in glo - rious hope! Our Lord the Judge shall come,

Re - joice, give thanks, and sing And tri - umph ev - er - more: Lift up your
When He had purged our stains He took His seat a - bove: Lift up your
And take His ser - vants up To their e - ter - nal home. Lift up your

heart, lift up your voice! Re - joice, a - gain I say, re - joice!
heart, lift up your voice! Re - joice, a - gain I say, re - joice!
heart, lift up your voice! Re - joice, a - gain I say, re - joice! A - men.

Words: Charles Wesley
Music: John Darwall

REJOICE—THE LORD IS KING!

After he had provided purification for sins, he sat
down at the right hand of the Majesty in heaven.
—Hebrews 1:3

THE TEXT OF "REJOICE—THE Lord Is King!" is one of the more than sixty-five hundred hymns written by Charles Wesley, the "sweet bard of Methodism."

Even though Wesley had had strict religious training in his youth, been educated at Oxford University, and done missionary service in the new colony of Georgia, he had no peace or joy in his heart and life. Returning to London after a discouraging time in America, he met with a group of Moravians in the Aldersgate hall and came to realize that salvation is by faith alone. In his journal entry for May 24, 1738, he wrote:

> At midnight I gave myself up to Christ; assured I was safe, sleeping or waking. Had continual experience of his power to overrule all temptation; and confessed, with joy and surprise, that he was able to do exceeding and abundantly for me, above what I can ask or think.[22]

In a spirit of joyous enthusiasm, Wesley began to write new hymns with increased fervor. He developed the hymn text of "Rejoice—the Lord Is King!" to encourage his followers to have a more spontaneous joy in their lives borne out of an awareness that Christ reigns victorious in heaven.

The hymn was based on the apostle Paul's instruction to the Christians at Philippi: "Rejoice in the Lord always. I will say it again: Rejoice!" (Philippians 4:4).

This instruction was written while Paul was a prisoner of Emperor Nero in Rome. The entire Philippian letter teaches that it is possible to be a victor in life—regardless of the circumstances—when one's faith is in an ascended, reigning Lord.

LIVING THE MELODY

"Rejoice in the Lord always" is easy to quote but difficult to practice. Yet we must remember that this attitude of joy is not an option for the Christian but a scriptural command. Whenever you struggle with praising God, meditate on the truth that our Lord is a reigning King, and try singing this hymn to train your brain toward gratitude.

What Scripture Says

Rejoice in the Lord always. I will say it again: Rejoice! . . . The Lord is near. Do not be anxious about anything, but in every situation, by prayer and petition, with thanksgiving, present your requests to God. And the peace of God, which transcends all understanding, will guard your hearts and your minds in Christ Jesus.

—Philippians 4:4–7

Since you have been raised to new life with Christ, set your sights on the realities of heaven, where Christ sits in the place of honor at God's right hand.

—Colossians 3:1 NLT

Wisdom from History

The soul that loves God has its rest in God and in God alone. In all the paths that men walk in in the world, they do not attain peace until they draw [near] to hope in God.[23]

—Isaac the Syrian (ca. 613–700)

Isaac the Syrian was a bishop and theologian whose writings on asceticism and the inner life were especially influential on Eastern Christianity.

Application Questions

- In what circumstances do you find it difficult to praise God?
- How might a fresh awareness that Christ reigns victorious in heaven help you to experience joy?

SING PRAISE TO GOD WHO REIGNS ABOVE

MIT FREUDEN ZART

JOHANN J. SCHÜTZ, 1640-1690
Trans. by Frances E. Cox, 1812-1897

From the Bohemian Brethren's
Kirchengesänge, 1566

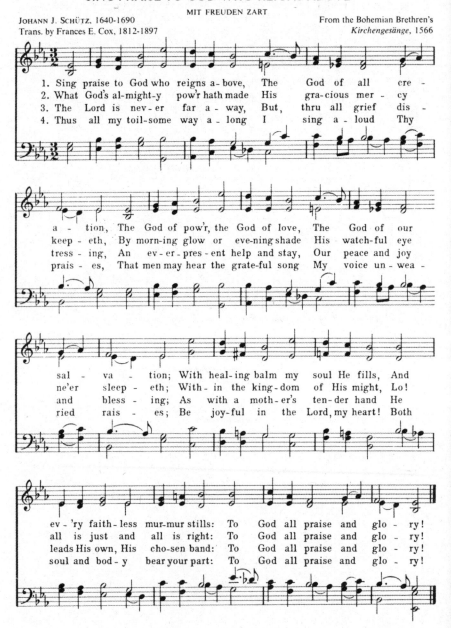

1. Sing praise to God who reigns a-bove, The God of all cre-
a - tion, The God of pow'r, the God of love, The God of our
sal - va - tion; With heal-ing balm my soul He fills, And
ev - 'ry faith-less mur-mur stills: To God all praise and glo - ry!

2. What God's al-might-y pow'r hath made His gra-cious mer-cy
keep - eth, By morn-ing glow or eve-ning shade His watch-ful eye
ne'er sleep - eth; With - in the king-dom of His might, Lo!
all is just and all is right: To God all praise and glo - ry!

3. The Lord is nev - er far a - way, But, thru all grief dis-
tress - ing, An ev - er - pres - ent help and stay, Our peace and joy
and bless - ing; As with a moth - er's ten-der hand He
leads His own, His cho-sen band: To God all praise and glo - ry!

4. Thus all my toil-some way a - long I sing a - loud Thy
prais - es, That men may hear the grate-ful song My voice un - wea -
ried rais - es; Be joy-ful in the Lord, my heart! Both
soul and bod - y bear your part: To God all praise and glo - ry!

— 17 —

SING PRAISE TO GOD
WHO REIGNS ABOVE

The LORD reigns, let the earth be glad;
let the distant shores rejoice.
—Psalm 97:1

FOLLOWING THE PROTESTANT REFORMATION AND Martin Luther's posting of the Ninety-Five Theses at the cathedral of Wittenberg in 1517, Lutheranism became the dominant religious force in Germany and throughout much of Europe.

In the seventeenth century, there was an important renewal movement within the Lutheran Church known as Pietism. The leader of this spiritual movement was a Lutheran pastor in Frankfurt, Germany, Philip J. Spener (1635–1705).

Mainly through prayer and Bible study cell groups, Spener sought to influence those who were Christian by name only and were accustomed to the dead orthodoxy that had taken over the church. Spener taught them the meaning of personal faith in Christ and the demands that such faith makes upon the believer for holy Christian living.

An important characteristic of the seventeenth-century Pietistic movement was the involvement of laymen. Many of the hymn writers and important voices in the church at this time came from all walks of life—including Johann J. Schutz, an authority in civil and canon law. He was closely allied with Spener in establishing small cell groups within the church. Schutz wrote a number of religious publications as well as five hymns. "Sing Praise to God Who Reigns Above" is his only hymn still in use.

LIVING THE MELODY

Isn't it a blessing to have men and women willing to challenge the status quo and dig deeply into Scripture to find out what God truly says? If you're not already part of one, consider joining a Bible study.

Spend some time today thanking God for the people in history who have given us a strong heritage of faith.

What Scripture Says

Keep this Book of the Law always on your lips; meditate on it day and night, so that you may be careful to do everything written in it. Then you will be prosperous and successful.

—Joshua 1:8

Surely God is my salvation;
    I will trust and not be afraid.
The LORD, the LORD himself, is my strength and my
        defense;
    he has become my salvation.

—Isaiah 12:2

Blessed is the one who reads aloud the words of this prophecy, and blessed are those who hear it and take to heart what is written in it, because the time is near.

—Revelation 1:3

Wisdom from History

[God is] too wise to err and too good to be unkind; [the Christian] trusts him where he cannot trace him.[24]

—Charles Spurgeon (1834–1892)

Spurgeon was a fiery, imaginative preacher. He had a sharp sense of humor and shrewd common sense that made him popular enough that the Metropolitan Tabernacle was built specifically to host the masses who came to hear him. But he was also a man of the people, founding a pastors' college, an orphanage, and an organization that brought good books and medical help door to door.

Application Questions

- How might you challenge the status quo in your own faith life?
- Is there a portion of Scripture you feel drawn to study?

STAND UP AND BLESS THE LORD

WALDEN S. M.

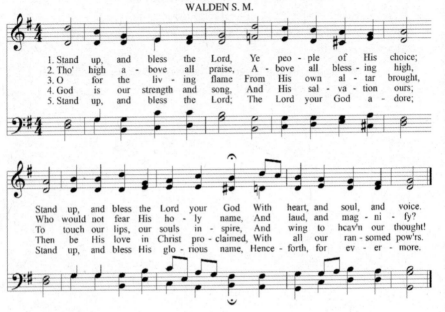

1. Stand up, and bless the Lord, Ye peo - ple of His choice;
2. Tho' high a - bove all praise, A - bove all bless - ing high,
3. O for the liv - ing flame From His own al - tar brought,
4. God is our strength and song, And His sal - va - tion ours;
5. Stand up, and bless the Lord; The Lord your God a - dore;

Stand up, and bless the Lord your God With heart, and soul, and voice.
Who would not fear His ho - ly name, And laud, and mag - ni - fy?
To touch our lips, our souls in - spire, And wing to heav'n our thought!
Then be His love in Christ pro - claimed, With all our ran - somed pow'rs.
Stand up, and bless His glo - rious name, Hence - forth, for ev - er - more.

Words: James Montgomery
Music: S. M. Bixby

— 18 —

STAND UP AND BLESS THE LORD

*Since we are receiving a kingdom that cannot be
shaken, let us be thankful, and so worship God
acceptably with reverence and awe.*
Hebrews 12:28

MANY EXCELLENT OPPORTUNITIES TO WITNESS for the Lord are lost each day simply because of our timidity. Perhaps we are with a group of colleagues when the Lord's name is blasphemed or the gospel derided . . . and we remain silent. How tragic that our noble words of praise on Sunday often leave us during the week when they are needed most.

"Stand Up and Bless the Lord" was written by James Montgomery in 1824 for a Sunday school anniversary. It was based on Nehemiah 9:5: "Stand up and praise the LORD your God, who is from everlasting to everlasting. Blessed be your glorious name, and may it be exalted above all blessing and praise."

Montgomery was the editor of a newspaper in Sheffield, England, and was known as an outspoken advocate for many humanitarian causes, especially the abolition of slavery. His ideas for social reform were considered so radical that he was imprisoned twice. Other causes he championed included hymn singing in the Anglican church services, foreign missions, and the British and Foreign Bible Society.

Montgomery wrote more than four hundred hymns, earning him a lasting place as one of England's finest hymn writers. May the challenge in "Stand Up and Bless the Lord" help you today.

LIVING THE MELODY

Refuse to be intimidated by those who seem hostile or indifferent to our Lord. Speak his praise graciously but boldly, and thank him for giving you opportunities to share your faith with others. Read a biography about a missionary or apologist to give you inspiration.

What Scripture Says

Open my lips, Lord,
and my mouth with declare your praise.
—Psalm 51:15

In your hearts revere Christ as Lord. Always be prepared to give an answer to everyone who asks you to give the reason for the hope that you have. But do this with gentleness and respect.
—1 Peter 3:15

My dear brothers and sisters, stand firm. Let nothing move you. Always give yourselves fully to the work of the Lord, because you know that your labor in the Lord is not in vain.
—1 Corinthians 15:58

Wisdom from History

The nature of God's love is unchangeable. Ours alternates all too readily. If it is our habit to love God with our own affection we shall turn cold towards Him whenever we are unhappy. . . . [Our own] affection ceases when the movement of emotion ceases; but a spiritual affection is strong, ever unrelenting, for it never relinquishes.[25]
—Watchman Nee (1903–1972)

Nee was the head of the dynamic movement known as the "Little Flock." This group forged a Christian witness for indigenous Chinese people independent of foreign missions and governmental influence. Nee spent twenty years in prison, where he refused to betray Christ and continued telling others about God.

Application Questions

- What holds you back from speaking up for Christ?
- How might you prepare to give an answer to those who ask about your faith?
- How would a focus on gratitude assist you in talking with others about God?

SURELY GOODNESS AND MERCY

John W. Peterson, 1921-
Alfred B. Smith, 1916-

John W. Peterson, 1921-
Alfred B. Smith, 1916-

1. A pil-grim was I, and a - wan-d'ring, In the cold night of
2. He re-stor-eth my soul when I'm wea - ry, He giv-eth me
3. When I walk thru the dark lone-some val - ley, My Sav - ior will

sin I did roam, When Je-sus the kind Shep-herd found me, And
strength day by day; He leads me be-side the still wa - ters, He
walk with me there; And safe-ly His great hand will lead me To the

CHORUS

now I am on my way home.
guards me each step of the way. Sure-ly good-ness and mer - cy shall
man-sions He's gone to pre - pare.

fol - low me All the days, all the days of my life; Sure-ly good-ness

and mer - cy shall fol - low me All the days, all the days of my life.

— 19 —

SURELY GOODNESS AND MERCY

*Answer me, LORD, out of the
goodness of your love;
in your great mercy turn to me.*
—Psalm 69:16

CHARLES HADDON SPURGEON, KNOWN AS the "Prince of Preachers" of the nineteenth century, labored for more than twenty years on his unrivaled commentary on the Psalms, a seven-volume work entitled *The Treasury of David*. Spurgeon observed that "only those who have meditated profoundly on the Psalms can have any adequate conception of the wealth they contain."[26] Consider this comment that Spurgeon made about Psalm 23, the basis of the hymn "Surely Goodness and Mercy":

> The sweetest word of the whole [psalm] is that monosyllable, *My*. He does not say, "The Lord is the shepherd of the world at large, and leadeth forth the multitude as His flock," but "The Lord is my shepherd"; if He be a shepherd to no one else, He is a shepherd to me; He cares for me, watches over me, and preserves me. The words are in the present tense. Whatever be the believer's position, he is even now under the pastoral care of Jehovah.[27]

John W. Peterson and Alfred B. Smith collaborated in 1958 to write "Surely Goodness and Mercy." Smith recalls the humorous touch that initially inspired this popular paraphrase of Psalm 23:

> It was written after receiving a letter from one of the descendants of P. P. Bliss, telling of Bliss's first country school

teacher, Miss Murphy, whom he dearly loved. It told of her teaching the class (before they could read or write) to memorize the Twenty-third Psalm. When the part "surely goodness and mercy" was reached, little Philip thought it said, "surely good Miss Murphy shall follow me all the days of my life." This little incident focused our thoughts on the phrase which became the heart and title of the song.

LIVING THE MELODY

Write out Psalm 23:1–3 (see below) on a card and post it somewhere you'll see it often—perhaps your bathroom mirror or under your computer monitor. Read it out loud several times a day, and carry its truth with you as you live in the joy and confidence of your heavenly Father's love and care for you.

What Scripture Says

The LORD is my shepherd, I lack nothing.
    He makes me lie down in green pastures,
he leads me beside quiet waters,
    he refreshes my soul.

          —Psalm 23:1–3

In your unfailing love you will lead
    the people you have redeemed.
In your strength you will guide them
    to your holy dwelling.

          —Exodus 15:13

Wisdom from History

To be grateful is to recognize the Love of God in everything He has given us—and He has given us everything. Every breath we draw is a gift of His love, every moment of existence is a grace, for it brings with it immense graces from Him.[28]

          —Thomas Merton (1915–1968)

Merton was an American monk, theologian, writer, and social activist who, during the tumultuous time of Vietnam, spoke openly on the topics of peace, racial tolerance, and social equality.

Application Questions
- Where have you seen God's care for you as an individual?
- What are some strategies that can help you see that God is with you in this very moment?

WHEN I SURVEY THE WONDROUS CROSS

HAMBURG

ISAAC WATTS, 1674-1748

From a Gregorian Chant
Arr. by Lowell Mason, 1792-1872

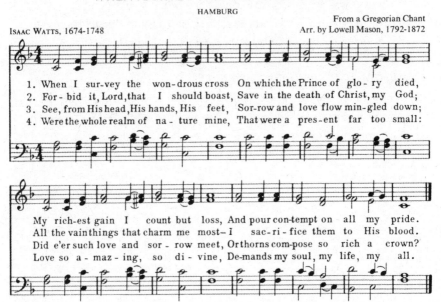

1. When I sur-vey the won-drous cross On which the Prince of glo - ry died,
2. For - bid it, Lord, that I should boast, Save in the death of Christ, my God;
3. See, from His head, His hands, His feet, Sor-row and love flow min-gled down;
4. Were the whole realm of na - ture mine, That were a pres-ent far too small:

My rich-est gain I count but loss, And pour con-tempt on all my pride.
All the vain things that charm me most—I sac-ri - fice them to His blood.
Did e'er such love and sor - row meet, Or thorns com-pose so rich a crown?
Love so a - maz - ing, so di - vine, De-mands my soul, my life, my all.

– 20 –

WHEN I SURVEY THE WONDROUS CROSS

Carrying his own cross, he went out to the place of the Skull (which in Aramaic is called Golgotha). There they crucified him.
—John 19:17–18

WHILE PREPARING FOR A COMMUNION service in 1707, Isaac Watts wrote "When I Survey the Wondrous Cross," a deeply moving, personal expression of gratitude for the amazing love that Christ's death on the cross revealed.

The hymn first appeared in print that same year in Watts's outstanding collection, *Hymns and Spiritual Songs*. The hymn was originally titled "Crucifixion to the World by the Cross of Christ." Noted theologian Matthew Arnold called it the greatest hymn in the English language.

Young Watts showed unusual talent at an early age, learning Latin when he was five, Greek at nine, French at eleven, and Hebrew at twelve. As he grew up, he became increasingly disturbed by the uninspiring psalm singing in the English churches. He wrote, "While we sing the praises of our God in his Church, we are employed in that part of worship which of all others is the nearest a-kin to heaven; and it is pity that this, of all others, should be performed the worst upon earth. . . . We are very much unacquainted with the songs of the New Jerusalem, and unpractised in the work of praise."[29]

In Watts's day, texts that expressed their author's personal feelings, like this one, were termed "hymns of human composure." They were controversial since almost all congregational singing at this time consisted of ponderous repetitions of the Psalms. The unique thoughts in Watts's lines pointed eighteenth-century Christians to a vivid and memorable view of the dying Savior—a view that surely must have led them to a deeper worship experience, as it does for us today.

Throughout his life, Watts wrote over six hundred hymns and is known today as the "father of English hymnody." His hymns were strong and triumphant statements of the Christian faith, yet none ever equaled the colorful imagery and genuine devotion of this emotionally stirring and magnificent hymn text.

LIVING THE MELODY

Our God is a God of reason and emotion. Today be grateful for a God who created us with the capacity to feel and be expressive. Take a moment to say, with Isaac Watts, "Lord, I give you 'my soul, my life, my all.'"

What Scripture Says

When we were utterly helpless, Christ came at just the right time and died for us sinners. Now, most people would not be willing to die for an upright person, though someone might perhaps be willing to die for a person who is especially good. But God showed his great love for us by sending Christ to die for us while we were still sinners. And since we have been made right in God's sight by the blood of Christ, he will certainly save us from God's condemnation. For since our friendship with God was restored by the death of his Son while we were still his enemies, we will certainly be saved through the life of his Son. So now we can rejoice in our wonderful new relationship with God because our Lord Jesus Christ has made us friends of God.

—Romans 5:6–11 NLT

Wisdom from History

God is a Person, and in the deep of His mighty nature He thinks, wills, enjoys, feels, loves, desires and suffers as any other person may. In making Himself known to us He stays by the familiar pattern of personality. He communicates with us through the avenues of our minds, our wills and our emotions. The continuous and unembarrassed interchange of love and thought between God and the soul of the redeemed man is the throbbing heart of the New Testament.[30]

—A. W. Tozer (1897–1963)

Tozer was an influential American pastor, magazine editor, and author. One of his most famous works is the Christian classic *The Pursuit of God*, in which he encourages the believer to cultivate a deep and personal relationship with God.

Application Questions
- How do your emotions help you connect to Christ?
- How does your logic help you in your faith walk?

GUIDE ME, O THOU GREAT JEHOVAH

CWM RHONDDA

WILLIAM WILLIAMS, 1717-1791
Trans. by Peter Williams, 1722-1796, and others

JOHN HUGHES, 1873-1932
Arr. by Norman Johnson, 1928-

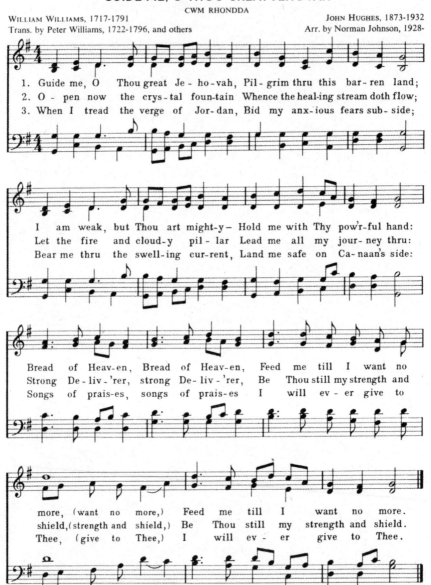

1. Guide me, O Thou great Je - ho - vah, Pil - grim thru this bar - ren land;
2. O - pen now the crys - tal foun - tain Whence the heal - ing stream doth flow;
3. When I tread the verge of Jor - dan, Bid my anx - ious fears sub - side;

I am weak, but Thou art might - y - Hold me with Thy pow'r - ful hand:
Let the fire and cloud - y pil - lar Lead me all my jour - ney thru:
Bear me thru the swell - ing cur - rent, Land me safe on Ca - naan's side:

Bread of Heav - en, Bread of Heav - en, Feed me till I want no
Strong De - liv - 'rer, strong De - liv - 'rer, Be Thou still my strength and
Songs of prais - es, songs of prais - es I will ev - er give to

more, (want no more,) Feed me till I want no more.
shield, (strength and shield,) Be Thou still my strength and shield.
Thee, (give to Thee,) I will ev - er give to Thee.

— 21 —

GUIDE ME, O THOU GREAT JEHOVAH

Since you are my rock and my fortress,
for the sake of your name lead and guide me.
—Psalm 31:3

"GUIDE ME, O THOU GREAT Jehovah" is one of the great hymns of the church on the subject of God's leading. It is a product of the revival that swept through Wales during the eighteenth century. This revival was led by a twenty-four-year-old Welsh preacher, Howell Harris, who stirred the land with his fervent evangelistic preaching and his use of congregational singing.

One of the lives touched by Harris's ministry was twenty-year-old William Williams. The son of a wealthy Welsh farmer, Williams was preparing to become a medical doctor. But upon hearing Harris's evangelistic challenge, Williams dedicated his life to God and Christian ministry. Williams, like Harris, decided to take all of Wales as his parish. For the next forty-three years, he traveled one hundred thousand miles on horseback, preaching and singing the gospel in his native tongue. He became known as the "sweet singer of Wales."

The vivid, symbolic imagery of "Guide Me, O Thou Great Jehovah" is drawn wholly from the Bible. The setting is the march of the Israelites from Egypt to Canaan. Although the Israelites' sin and unbelief kept them from their destination for forty years, God provided for their physical needs with a new supply of manna each day (Exodus 16).

During the Hebrews' years of wandering, they became faint from lack of water. At the command of God, Moses struck a large rock with his wooden staff. Out of it flowed a pure, crystalline stream that preserved their lives (Exodus 17:1–7). God also continued to guide them with a pillar of cloud by day and a pillar of fire by night (Exodus 13:21–22).

The need for daily guidance is still one of the greatest for the believer. How easily our lives can go astray without the assurance of divine leadership.

LIVING THE MELODY

Make a habit of asking God for your daily portion of his wisdom and strength. Claim God's promises for your life in even the small decisions you will need to make today. Note his presence throughout the day, and give thanks for his daily practical provision.

What Scripture Says
> You will show me the path of life;
> In Your presence is fullness of joy;
> At Your right hand are pleasures forevermore.
> —Psalm 16:11 NKJV

> The LORD will guide you continually,
> And satisfy your soul in drought,
> And strengthen your bones;
> You shall be like a watered garden,
> And like a spring of water, whose waters do not fail.
> —Isaiah 58:11 NKJV

Wisdom from History
> God has promised to supply our needs. What we don't have now we don't need now.[31]
> —Elisabeth Elliot (1926–2015)

Elliot was a missionary whose first husband, Jim Elliot, sought to evangelize the Waorani people of eastern Ecuador and was later killed. She remained in Ecuador as a missionary for years after her husband's death.

Application Questions

- What are some of God's promises of provision? How might releasing responsibility to God help ease anxiety and fear?
- What do you need God's wisdom and provision for today?

BLESSED BE THE NAME

1. All praise to Him who reigns a - bove, In maj - es - ty su - preme;
2. His name a - bove all names shall stand, Ex - alt - ed more and more,
3. Re - deem - er, Sav - ior, Friend of man Once ru - ined by the fall;

Who gave His Son for man to die, That He might man re - deem.
At God the Fa - ther's own right hand Where an - gels hosts a - dore.
Thou hast de - vised sal - va - tion's plan, For Thou hast died for all.

Chorus

Bless - ed be the name, bless - ed be the name, Bless - ed be the name of the Lord;

Bless - ed be the name, bless - ed be the name, Bless - ed be the name of the Lord.

Words by William. H. Clark
Music: Ralph E. Hudson, Arr. by William J. Kirkpatrick

– 22 –

BLESSED BE THE NAME

I will exalt you, my God the King;
I will praise your name for ever and ever.
—Psalm 145:1

THE BIBLE TEACHES THAT OUR Lord honors two things above all else: his name and his word (Psalm 138:2 ESV). These two priorities should also be the most sacred trusts in our spiritual lives. A name is an individual's main identification and the carrier of his or her reputation.

In the Bible, God renamed individuals—for instance, Jacob to Israel and Simon to Peter (Genesis 32:24–28; John 1:42)—to reflect more accurately their changed identities. It is only natural, then, to defend one's name at all costs.

To many people today, the names "Jesus" and "God" are merely words to use in blasphemy. For those of us who associate those names with divine love, such talk cannot be dismissed lightly. Christ himself spoke out against becoming sacrilegious in our speaking when he cautioned his disciples never to swear either by heaven or earth (Matthew 5:34–37). And it should be remembered that one-tenth of the moral law deals with profaning God's name and gives this serious warning: "The LORD will not hold anyone guiltless who misuses his name" (Deuteronomy 5:11). Even our approach to the heavenly Father in prayer must always be done with reverence—in the name of Jesus (John 16:23).

Let us determine to use this day to truly magnify his name and proclaim his worth together.

The stanzas of "Blessed Be the Name" first appeared in 1891 in *Hymns of the Christian Life.* The melody was likely one of the early folk hymn tunes used in nineteenth-century camp meetings. The stanzas were written by W. H. Clark, and the refrain was written by Ralph E. Hudson.

LIVING THE MELODY

As bearers of the divine name—as *Christians*—we are messengers of who God is. Using a list of God's various names, find ways you can show those aspects of God's character to the world around you. For example, since God is a God who sees (El Roi), notice the people on the margins of society and make them feel known. By exhibiting God's characteristics, we exalt his name.

What Scripture Says

LORD, our Lord,
how majestic is your name in all the earth!

You have set your glory
in the heavens.
—Psalm 8:1

Glorify the LORD with me;
let us exalt his name together.
—Psalm 34:3

I am the LORD; that is my name!
I will not yield my glory to another
or my praise to idols.
—Isaiah 42:8

Wisdom from History

"This is My commandment, that ye love one another as I have loved you." We cannot approach that, much less pass it; so we cannot love too much. . . . Only let the love be selfless, strong, brave, faithful.[33]
—Amy Carmichael (1867–1951)

Carmichael was an Irish missionary to India who, despite almost constant physical pain, opened an orphanage and founded an organization whose mission was partly to rescue temple children who'd been forced into slavery.

Application Questions
- What does being a Christian mean to you?
- How can you show God's characteristics to those around you?

HOLY GOD, WE PRAISE THY NAME

1. Ho - ly God, we praise Your name, Lord of all, we
2. Hark! the loud ce - les - tial hymn an - gel choirs a -
3. Lo! the ap - os - tol - ic train join Your sa - cred
4. Ho - ly Fa - ther, Ho - ly Son, Ho - ly Spir - it,

bow be - fore You; All on earth Your scep - ter claim,
bove are rais - ing; Cher - u - bim and ser - a - phim
name to hal - low; Proph - ets swell the glad re - frain,
three we name You; While in es - sence on - ly one,

all in heav - en a - bove a - dore You; In - fi - nite Your
in un - ceas - ing cho - rus prais - ing, Fill the heav - ens with
and the white - robed mar - tyrs fol - low; And from morn to
un - di - vid - ed God we claim You, Then, a - dor - ing,

vast do - main, ev - er last - ing is Your reign.
sweet ac - cord; ho - ly, ho - ly, ho - ly Lord.
set of sun, thru the church the song goes on.
bend the knee, and con - fess the mys - ter - y.

Words: Ignaz Franz, Tr. by Clarence A. Walworth
Music: Katholishches Gesagbuch

— 23 —

HOLY GOD, WE PRAISE THY NAME

In God we make our boast all day long,
and we will praise your name forever.
—Psalm 44:8

KNOWN IN LATIN AS *Te Deum Laudamus* ("God, We Praise You"), the hymn "Holy God, We Praise Thy Name" has been one of the supreme triumphal expressions of praise used by the Christian church throughout the centuries.

The origin of this noble expression of praise and worship is obscure. The original score of *Te Deum Laudamus* was likely composed by an important leader in the development of early church music, Saint Ambrose, in AD 387. Paraphrases of the fourth-century *Te Deum* were written in many languages, including in German by Ignaz Franz, from which our present English text was translated by the American Catholic priest Clarence A. Walworth.

The hymn is still an important part of the morning service liturgy in Anglican churches, and it is sung frequently in many Protestant churches as well.

The fourth stanza is one of the strongest hymn affirmations of the doctrine of the triune Godhead. The Trinity was at the center of a large controversy in the early church. Arius (ca. AD 250–336), to whom the founding of Arianism is attributed, maintained that "if the Father was God, then the Son was a creature of the Father"—a middle Being between God and the world, divine but not to be worshiped as God. At the Council of Alexandria (AD 321) and later at the First Council of Nicaea (AD 325), this teaching was thoroughly branded as heresy. However, this controversy on the person and deity of Christ has continued even to the present time in the teachings of various cults.

LIVING THE MELODY

Praising God's name may seem like an odd concept at the outset—that someone's actual name should be given glory. However, if we study the names of God in Scripture, we will realize we have much to be thankful for. For example, we have a God who sees us (El Roi). He is the Lord God Almighty (El Shaddai), the Everlasting God (El Olam), and the Lord who will provide (Jehovah Jireh).

Take time today to research some of the names of God. Read the biblical stories associated with them. Then praise God for fulfilling the meaning behind those names.

What Scripture Says

Praise be to his glorious name forever;
> may the whole earth be filled with his glory.
> > —Psalm 72:19

Yours, LORD, is the greatness and the power
> and the glory and the majesty and the splendor,
> for everything in heaven and earth is yours.
Yours, LORD, is the kingdom;
> you are exalted as head over all.
> > —1 Chronicles 29:11

Wisdom from History

Names tell stories, most of all the name which is above all other names, the name of Jesus. In his name I am called to live. His name has become my house, my dwelling place, my refuge, my ark. His name has to start telling the story of being born, growing up, growing old, and dying—revealing a God who loved us so much that he sent his only child to us.[32]
> —Henri Nouwen (1932–1996)

Nouwen was a priest, author, and teacher. He also served a community of individuals with intellectual and developmental disabilities at L'Arche Daybreak in Canada. He wrote extensively about learning to live as the beloved of God.

Application Questions

- How does knowing someone's name affect how you see that person?
- How does knowing some of God's names help you see him more clearly?

BLESSED REDEEMER

Avis B. Christiansen, 1895-

Harry Dixon Loes, 1892-1965

1. Up Cal-v'ry's moun-tain, one dread-ful morn, Walked Christ my Sav-ior,
2. "Fa-ther, for-give them!" thus did He pray, E'en while His life-blood
3. O how I love Him, Sav-ior and Friend! How can my prais-es

wea-ry and worn; Fac-ing for sin-ners death on the cross,
flowed fast a-way; Pray-ing for sin-ners while in such woe—
ev-er find end! Thru years un-num-bered on heav-en's shore,

That He might save them from end-less loss.
No one but Je-sus ev-er loved so.
My tongue shall praise Him for-ev-er-more.

CHORUS

Bless-ed Re-deem-er, pre-cious Re-deem-er! Seems now I see Him on Cal-va-ry's tree, Wound-ed and bleed-ing, for sin-ners plead-ing—Blind and un-heed-ing— dy-ing for me!

− 24 −

BLESSED REDEEMER

*When they came to the place called the Skull, they
crucified him there, along with the criminals—one
on his right, the other on his left.*
—Luke 23:33

IT IS THOUGHT THAT THE day we call "Good Friday" originated
from the term "God's Friday," as it was the day Christ was led to the
hill of Golgotha and crucified, assuring an eternal reconciliation for
lost people.

The Roman cross, intended to be an instrument of cruel death,
instead became an instrument of new life and hope for the human
race. God loved and valued each of us so highly that he willingly paid
the greatest price imaginable for our salvation.

The composer Harry Dixon Loes was a popular music teacher
at the Moody Bible Institute from 1939 until his death in 1965.
Long before his time at Moody, while listening one day to a sermon
on the subject of Christ's atonement entitled "Blessed Redeemer,"
Loes was inspired to compose a tune of the same name. He then
sent his melody with its suggested title to Avis B. Christiansen, a
friend of many years, asking her to write the text. The completed
hymn first appeared in the hymnal *Songs of Redemption* in 1920.

Christiansen, one of the important gospel hymn writers of the
twentieth century, wrote hundreds of gospel hymn texts as well as
several volumes of published poems out of her own experience of a
daily walk and intimate fellowship with the Lord. Throughout her
long lifetime of ninety years, she collaborated with many well-known
gospel musicians to contribute several other choice hymns to our
hymnals, such as "Blessed Calvary" and "I Know I'll See Jesus Some
Day."

LIVING THE MELODY

We have a God who loves us and sacrificed for us. Today take a moment to be thankful that the powerful God who created the world is also the same God who stooped low enough to meet us where we are. Since Christ has paid the price of our redemption in full, all we have to do is believe, receive, and rejoice.

What Scripture Says

When you were dead in your sins and in the uncircumcision of your flesh, God made you alive with Christ. He forgave us all our sins, having canceled the charge of our legal indebtedness, which stood against us and condemned us; he has taken it away, nailing it to the cross. And having disarmed the powers and authorities, he made a public spectacle of them, triumphing over them by the cross.

—Colossians 2:13–15

In him we have redemption through his blood, the forgiveness of sins, in accordance with the riches of God's grace that he lavished on us.

—Ephesians 1:7–8

Wisdom from History

One thing is certain: if He was God and nothing else, His immortality means nothing to us; if He was man and no more, His death is no more important than yours or mine. But if He really was both God and man, then when the man Jesus died, God died too; and when the God Jesus rose from the dead, man rose too, because they were one and the same person.[34]

—Dorothy L. Sayers (1893–1957)

Sayers was an English crime novelist, essayist, and playwright with a passion for Christian apologetics.

Application Questions

- Does knowing that God loves you deeply help you trust him? Why or why not?
- What does it mean to you that even the cross can be redeemed by God?

HE LEADETH ME

Joseph H. Gilmore, 1834-1918

William B. Bradbury, 1816-1868

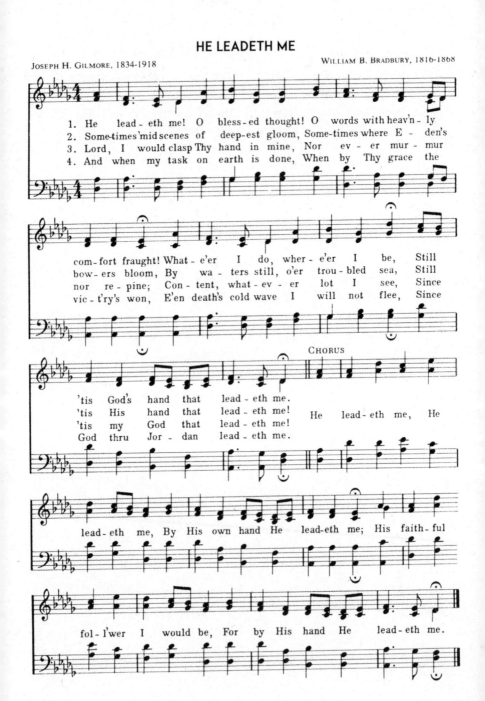

1. He lead-eth me! O bless-ed thought! O words with heav'n-ly
2. Some-times 'mid scenes of deep-est gloom, Some-times where E - den's
3. Lord, I would clasp Thy hand in mine, Nor ev - er mur - mur
4. And when my task on earth is done, When by Thy grace the

com-fort fraught! What - e'er I do, wher - e'er I be, Still
bow - ers bloom, By wa - ters still, o'er trou - bled sea, Still
nor re - pine; Con - tent, what - ev - er lot I see, Since
vic - t'ry's won, E'en death's cold wave I will not flee, Since

CHORUS

'tis God's hand that lead - eth me.
'tis His hand that lead - eth me! He lead - eth me, He
'tis my God that lead - eth me!
God thru Jor - dan lead - eth me.

lead - eth me, By His own hand He lead-eth me; His faith-ful

fol - l'wer I would be, For by His hand He lead-eth me.

— 25 —

HE LEADETH ME

He makes me lie down in green pastures,
he leads me beside quiet waters,
he refreshes my soul.
—Psalm 23:2–3

THE BLESSEDNESS AND AWE OF being led by Almighty God himself so affected the author of "He Leadeth Me" that he wrote its beloved words spontaneously—and those exact words have been sung by believers around the world for more than a century.

Although Joseph H. Gilmore became a distinguished university and seminary professor, an author of several textbooks on Hebrew and English literature, and a respected Baptist minister, he is best remembered today for this one hymn, hurriedly written when he was just twenty-eight. Gilmore scribbled down its lines while visiting with friends after preaching about the truths of Psalm 23 at a Wednesday evening service at First Baptist Church in Philadelphia. He left this account:

> At the close of the service we adjourned to Deacon Watson's pleasant home, where we were being entertained. During our conversation the blessedness of God's leading so grew upon me that I took out my pencil, wrote the text just as it stands today, handed it to my wife, and thought no more of it.

Without telling her husband, Mrs. Gilmore sent the verses to the *Watchman and Reflector* magazine, where it first appeared the following year. Three years later, Joseph Gilmore went to Rochester,

New York, as a candidate to become the pastor of Second Baptist Church. He recalls,

> Upon entering the chapel I took up a hymnal, thinking—I wonder what they sing here. To my amazement the book opened up at "He Leadeth Me," and that was the first time I knew that my hurriedly written lines had found a place among the songs of the church.

William B. Bradbury, an important American contributor to early gospel hymnody, added two additional lines to the chorus: "His faithful foll'wer I would be / for by His hand He leadeth me." Does that describe you?

LIVING THE MELODY

Find a quiet place where you can sit and relax. Close your eyes. Visualize your loving God walking a beautiful path with you, comforting you, laughing with you, protecting you, enjoying the time he has with you. Now reach out and hold his hand as he helps you step over whatever struggles you're experiencing. Thank him for leading you well.

What Scripture Says
> If I rise on the wings of the dawn,
>   if I settle on the far side of the sea,
> even there your hand will guide me,
>   your right hand will hold me fast.
> If I say, "Surely the darkness will hide me
>   and the light become night around me,"
> even the darkness will not be dark to you;
>   the night will shine like the day,
>   for darkness is as light to you.
>   —Psalm 139:9–12

Wisdom from History

Thank you, Lord: how many rich people are in prison wearing irons at present; how many more have their feet fastened to wood, not being able so much as to satisfy their bodily needs—whereas I am like a king with my legs stretched out.[35]

—A Desert Father

The Desert Fathers started living in the deserts of Egypt as ascetics and hermits around the time of the third century. Instead of becoming martyrs, they chose to sacrifice their lives by giving up worldly comforts and embracing austerity and solitude, depending solely on God's provision.

Application Questions

- Is it easy for you to follow God on your life's path? Why or why not?
- How have you been blessed by God's leading?

MAKE ME A BLESSING

1. Out in the high - ways and by - ways of life, Man - y are wea - ry
2. Tell the sweet sto - ry of Christ and His love, Tell of His pow'r to
3. Give as 'twas giv - en to you in your need, Love as the Mas - ter

and sad;
are wea - ry and sad;
for - give;
His pow'r to for - give;
loved you;
the Mas - ter loved you;

Car - ry the sun - shine where dark - ness is rife,
Oth - ers will trust Him if on - ly you prove
Be to the help - less a help - er in - deed,

Chorus

Mak - ing the sor - row - ing glad.
True, ev - 'ry mo - ment you live.
Un - to your mis - sion be true.

Make me a bless - ing, Make me a

bless - ing, Out of my life
Out of my life

may Je - sus shine; Make me a bless - ing,

Words: Ira B. Wilson
Music: George S. Schuler

MAKE ME A BLESSING

Through the blessing of the upright
a city is exalted,
but by the mouth of the wicked
it is destroyed.
—Proverbs 11:11

THE COMMAND OF SCRIPTURE IS that we produce fruit. Jesus said, "This is to my Father's glory, that you bear much fruit, showing yourselves to be my disciples" (John 15:8). Regardless of the task God calls us to, whether great or small, he promises to bless it when we do it faithfully and with sincere motives. The Scriptures also teach that our deeds of compassion and mercy must be done with cheerfulness, never simply out of duty (Romans 12:8). Saint Francis of Assisi purportedly said, "It is not fitting, when one is in God's service, to have a gloomy face or a chilling look." Representing Christ and serving others must become a normal, happy way of life as we "carry the sunshine where darkness is rife."

The text of "Make Me a Blessing" was written in 1909 by Ira B. Wilson. A musician associated for many years with the Lorenz Publishing Company, he served as editor of the popular periodicals *Choir Leader* and *Choir Herald*. The music for the hymn was added fifteen years later by George Schuler, who served for more than forty years in the music department of the Moody Bible Institute. Throughout his lifetime Schuler contributed much fine music for both vocal and keyboard use.

"Make Me a Blessing" was first introduced in 1924 at a Sunday school convention in Cleveland, Ohio, where Schuler had one thousand copies of the song printed for the occasion. It was received with much enthusiasm, and its words have since been widely used to challenge believers to make their lives useful to God.

LIVING THE MELODY

Our service to and love for others can be a way of saying thank you to a God who cares deeply for us. Though he doesn't require our help, we have the privilege and joy of participating in the fulfillment of God's plan for others around us. Today look for a way to speak a kind word or help someone in a small way, and give glory to God for the gifts he has given you.

What Scripture Says

Then I heard the Lord asking, "Whom should I send as a messenger to this people? Who will go for us?

I said, "Here I am. Send me."

—Isaiah 6:8 NLT

You are the light of the world—like a city on a hilltop that cannot be hidden. No one lights a lamp and then puts it under a basket. Instead, a lamp is placed on a stand, where it gives light to everyone in the house. In the same way, let your good deeds shine out for all to see, so that everyone will praise your heavenly Father.

—Matthew 5:14–16 NLT

He comforts us in all our troubles so that we can comfort others. When they are troubled, we will be able to give them the same comfort God has given us.

—2 Corinthians 1:4 NLT

Wisdom from History

What is the kingdom of Christ? A rule of love, of truth—a rule of service. The king is the chief servant in it.[36]

—George MacDonald (1824–1905)

MacDonald was a Scottish author, poet, and minister who was one of the pioneers of the modern fantasy genre and a major influence on Lewis Carroll, C. S. Lewis, Ray Bradbury, Flannery O'Connor, and a host of others.

Application Questions

- How are you using your giftings to show God to others?
- How do you feel when you help others?

A CHILD OF THE KING

1. My Fa - ther is rich in hous - es and lands, He hold - eth the
2. My Fa - ther's own Son, the Sav - ior of men, Once wan - dered o'er
3. I once was an out - cast stran - ger of earth, A sin - ner by
4. A tent or a cot - tage, why should I care? They're build - ing a

wealth of the world in His hands! Of ru - bies and dia - monds, of
earth as the poor - est of them; But now He is reign - ing in
choice, an al - ien by birth! But I've been a - dopt - ed, my
pal - ace for me o - ver there! Tho' here I'm a stran - ger yet

sil - ver and gold, His cof - fers are full,- He has rich - es un - told.
glo - ry on high, Pre - par - ing a place for the sweet by and by.
name's writ - ten down,- An heir to a man - sion, a robe and a crown.
still I may sing: All glo - ry to God, I'm a child of the King!

Chorus

I'm a child of the King, A child of the King!

Rit...

With Je - sus my Sav - ior, I'm a child of the King.

Words by Hattie E. Buell
Music by John B. Sumner

– 27 –

A CHILD OF THE KING

We are God's children. Now if we are children, then
we are heirs—heirs of God and co-heirs with Christ,
if indeed we share in his sufferings in order that we
may also share in his glory.
—Romans 8:16–17

As CHILDREN OF THE HEAVENLY kingdom and heirs of God's riches, we possess abundant spiritual blessings.

- We have been justified and made acceptable to God (Romans 5:1).
- We have been adopted into God's royal family (Romans 8:16–17).
- We have been given citizenship in heaven (Philippians 3:20).
- We possess the indwelling Holy Spirit (1 Corinthians 6:19).
- We have been brought into the kingdom of the Son of God (Colossians 1:13).
- We have the promise that the best is yet to come, a heavenly home (1 Corinthians 2:9).

Whether you are great or small in the eyes of the world, you are still God's child. An infant is truly a child of its parents, and so is a full-grown person. You are as dear to your heavenly Father as the most prominent member in his family.

Harriett E. Buell wrote the words for "A Child of the King" while walking home from her Sunday church service. She sent her text to the *Northern Christian Advocate*, and it was printed in the February 1, 1877, issue of the newspaper. John Sumner, a singing school music teacher, saw the words and composed the music.

The hymn has been widely used since then to remind believers who they really are—bearers of God's image (Genesis 1:26) and children of the King of Kings.

LIVING THE MELODY

Not only has God paid the price for all the wrong things we have done and the right things we haven't done, but he has also gifted us beyond measure. Read back through the list of benefits of choosing God as the king of your life and thank him for each one. Bring a sense of amazement into your day. We are children of the Most High and heirs to the overflowing riches of his kingdom.

What Scripture Says

Those who are led by the Spirit of God are the children of God. The Spirit you received does not make you slaves, so that you live in fear again; rather, the Spirit you received brought about your adoption to sonship. And by him we cry, "*Abba*, Father." The Spirit himself testifies with our spirit that we are God's children. Now if we are children, then we are heirs—heirs of God and co-heirs with Christ, if indeed we share in his sufferings in order that we may also share in his glory.

—Romans 8:14–17

Listen to me, dear brothers and sisters. Hasn't God chosen the poor in this world to be rich in faith? Aren't they the ones who will inherit the Kingdom he promised to those who love him?

—James 2:5 NLT

Wisdom from History

This king, full of mercy and goodness, very far from chastening me, embraces me with love, invites me to feast at his table, serves me with his own hands, and gives me the key to his treasures. He converses with me, and takes delight in me, and treats me as if I were his favorite.[37]

       —Brother Lawrence (1611–1691)

Brother Lawrence was a lay brother in a monastery in Paris. During his life, he made an effort to live every mundane moment in "the presence of God." He found ways to transform every trivial chore into a glorious experience of heaven.

Application Questions

- Which of the blessings listed at the beginning of this devotion means the most to you right now? Why?
- How does knowing that you are a beloved child of the King affect you?

FOR THE BEAUTY OF THE EARTH

Folliott S. Pierpoint, 1835-1917

DIX

Conrad Kocher, 1786-1872

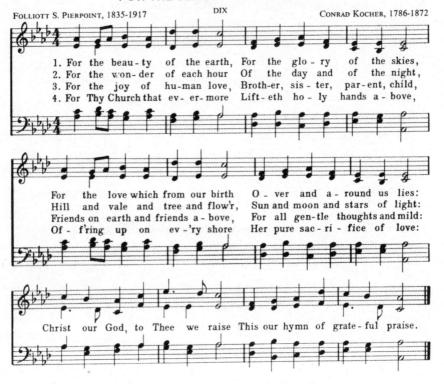

1. For the beau-ty of the earth, For the glo-ry of the skies,
2. For the won-der of each hour Of the day and of the night,
3. For the joy of hu-man love, Broth-er, sis-ter, par-ent, child,
4. For Thy Church that ev-er-more Lift-eth ho-ly hands a-bove,

For the love which from our birth O-ver and a-round us lies:
Hill and vale and tree and flow'r, Sun and moon and stars of light:
Friends on earth and friends a-bove, For all gen-tle thoughts and mild:
Of-f'ring up on ev-'ry shore Her pure sac-ri-fice of love:

Christ our God, to Thee we raise This our hymn of grate-ful praise.

– 28 –

FOR THE BEAUTY OF THE EARTH

*Whatever is true, whatever is noble, whatever is
right, whatever is pure, whatever is lovely,
whatever is admirable—if anything is excellent or
praiseworthy—think about such things.*
—Philippians 4:8

ONE OF THE DELIGHTS WE as adults experience in being around
children is hearing their delighted squeals as they discover some or-
dinary object. No doubt our heavenly Father is also pleased when his
children take time to observe and appreciate his creation and then
express joyous gratitude to him for his countless blessings.

The hymn "For the Beauty of the Earth" reminds us of life's common blessings we so often take for granted—the beauties of nature,
our parents, family, friends, church. The lyrics direct us to God, the
giver of every good and perfect gift.

Not much is known about Folliott Sandford Pierpoint, author
of this lovely text. He was born in the intriguing old town of Bath,
England, in 1835. Following his graduation from Queen's College,
Cambridge, he taught the classics for a time at Somerset College,
and he later became an independent writer. Although he published
seven volumes of poems and hymn texts, many of them showing his
love of nature, he is best remembered for this beautiful hymn.

The inspiration for Pierpoint's hymn text is said to have come to
the young author as he strolled about his native town one day in the
late spring, entranced by the beautiful countryside with the winding
Avon River in the distance. His heart no doubt swelled up within
him as he enjoyed the beauties of God's creation—the sun, the flow-
ers, the birds.

Pierpoint also recalled his social blessings—friends and family, those relationships that bring such enriching dimensions to our lives. Above all, however, were the spiritual blessings as represented by the church, God's chosen agency for accomplishing his divine purposes in the world. For all these blessings, Pierpoint directs our gratitude to Christ with a "hymn of grateful praise."

LIVING THE MELODY

Did you know that celebration is one of the spiritual disciplines? Practicing celebration allows us to experience awe at God's blessings and strengthens our faith. Consider planning a celebration. It could be for a milestone in your life, or for a change in season, or for a sporting event . . . or for no reason at all. Invite your family, friends, and coworkers, and give everyone the opportunity to thank God for the common blessings we often ignore. Keep the celebration simple—no need to be fancy; all that matters is being present with your guests.

What Scripture Says

I will praise you, LORD, with all my heart;
   I will tell of all the marvelous things you have done.
I will be filled with joy because of you.
   I will sing praises to your name, O Most High.
                                        —Psalm 9:1–2 NLT

Every good and perfect gift is from above, coming down from the Father of the heavenly lights, who does not change like shifting shadows.
                                        —James 1:17

Wisdom from History

The Christian should be an alleluia from head to foot.[38]
                        —Saint Augustine of Hippo (354–430)

Saint Augustine was a theologian, philosopher, and bishop of Hippo. Hailing from North Africa, Augustine had a profound impact on Christian faith, especially relating to salvation and divine grace.

Application Questions

- What is something you can celebrate today? Perhaps an accomplishment, a choice, a narrow miss, even the air in your lungs?
- Does celebration come naturally to you? Why or why not?

GREAT IS THY FAITHFULNESS

Thomas O. Chisholm, 1866-1960

William M. Runyan, 1870-1957

1. Great is Thy faith-ful-ness, O God my Fa-ther! There is no
2. Sum-mer and win-ter, and spring-time and har-vest, Sun, moon and
3. Par-don for sin and a peace that en-dur-eth, Thine own dear

shad-ow of turn-ing with Thee; Thou chang-est not, Thy com-
stars in their cours-es a-bove, Join with all na-ture in
pres-ence to cheer and to guide, Strength for to-day and bright

pas-sions, they fail not: As Thou hast been Thou for-ev-er wilt be.
man-i-fold wit-ness To Thy great faith-ful-ness, mer-cy and love.
hope for to-mor-row— Bless-ings all mine, with ten thou-sand be-side!

CHORUS

Great is Thy faith-ful-ness! Great is Thy faith-ful-ness! Morn-ing by

morn-ing new mer-cies I see; All I have need-ed Thy

hand hath pro-vid-ed— Great is Thy faith-ful-ness, Lord, un-to me!

— 29 —

GREAT IS THY FAITHFULNESS

*Because of the LORD's great
love we are not consumed,
for his compassions never fail.
They are new every morning;
great is your faithfulness.*
—Lamentations 3:22–23

ONE OF THE IMPORTANT LESSONS the children of Israel had to learn during their wilderness journey was that God's provision of manna for them came on a morning-by-morning basis. Manna could not be stored for future use (Exodus 16:19–21).

While many enduring hymns are born out of a particular dramatic experience, "Great Is Thy Faithfulness" was simply the result of Thomas Obadiah Chisholm's morning-by-morning realization of God's personal faithfulness in his daily life. In a letter dated 1941, he wrote:

> My income has never been large at any time due to impaired health in the earlier years which has followed me on until now. But I must not fail to record here the unfailing faithfulness of a covenant keeping God and that He has given me many wonderful displays of His providing care which have filled me with astonishing gratefulness.

Chisholm was born in a humble log cabin in Franklin, Kentucky. From this humble beginning and without the benefit of high school or advanced education, he somehow became a schoolteacher at the age of sixteen in the same country school where he had received his elementary training. When he was twenty-one, he became the associate editor of his hometown weekly newspaper, the *Franklin Favorite*. After accepting Christ as Savior six years later, he became editor of the *Pentecostal Herald* and later was ordained as a Methodist minister.

Throughout his long lifetime, Chisholm wrote more than twelve hundred sacred poems, many of which have since become prominent hymn texts.

LIVING THE MELODY

We have a God who promises to never leave us or forsake us. He is the very definition of faithful and steadfast, no matter the season. Be encouraged today that he does what he promises. Every morning carries new mercies from God (Lamentations 3:22–23). If you're struggling today, look up an audio version of "Great Is Thy Faithfulness," and let praise to God wash over you to help you see God in your moment-by-moment life.

What Scripture Says

Your unfailing love, O LORD, is as vast as the heavens;
    your faithfulness reaches beyond the clouds.
Your righteousness is like the mighty mountains,
    your justice like the ocean depths.
You care for people and animals alike, O LORD.
    How precious is your unfailing love, O God!
All humanity finds shelter
    in the shadow of your wings.
                                        —Psalm 36:5–7 NLT

Be glad, people of Zion,
    rejoice in the Lord your God,
for he has given you the autumn rains
    because he is faithful.
He sends you abundant showers,

both autumn and spring rains, as before.
—Joel 2:23

Wisdom from History

"Taste and know that the Lord is bountiful" (Ps. 34:8). For He is the jubilation of the righteous, the joy of the upright, the gladness of the humble, and the solace of those who grieve because of Him.[39]
—Saint Gregory Palamas (1296–1359)

Saint Gregory Palamas was a Byzantine Greek theologian and archbishop of Thessaloniki. He supported the monastic tradition of hesychasm—repetitive contemplative prayer as a means of finding divine quietness and union with God.

Application Questions

- How does knowledge of God's faithfulness help you be stead-fast in your moment-by-moment life?
- What is your favorite season—spring, summer, fall, or winter? How do you see God in that season?

IT IS WELL WITH MY SOUL

Horatio G. Spafford, 1828-1888

Philip P. Bliss, 1838-1876

1. When peace, like a riv - er, at - tend - eth my way, When sor - rows like
2. Tho Sa - tan should buf - fet, tho tri - als should come, Let this blest as -
3. My sin— O the bliss of this glo - ri - ous tho't— My sin, not in
4. And, Lord, haste the day when my faith shall be sight, The clouds be rolled

sea - bil - lows roll— What - ev - er my lot, Thou hast taught me to say,
sur - ance con - trol, That Christ hath re - gard - ed my help - less es - tate,
part, but the whole, Is nailed to the cross, and I bear it no more:
back as a scroll: The trump shall re - sound and the Lord shall de - scend,

Chorus

It is well, it is well with my soul.
And hath shed His own blood for my soul. It is well
Praise the Lord, praise the Lord, O my soul! It is well
"E - ven so"— it is well with my soul.

with my soul, It is well, it is well with my soul.
with my soul,

— 30 —

IT IS WELL WITH MY SOUL

God is our refuge and strength,
an ever-present help in trouble.
—Psalm 46:1

INNER PEACE THROUGH AN IMPLICIT trust in God's love is the real evidence of a mature Christian faith. Only with this kind of confidence in his heavenly Father could Horatio G. Spafford experience such heartrending tragedies as he did and yet be able to say, "It is well with my soul."

Spafford had known peaceful and happy days as a successful attorney in Chicago. He was the father of four daughters, an active member of the Presbyterian church, and a loyal friend and supporter of D. L. Moody and other evangelical leaders of his day. Then a series of calamities began, starting with the Great Chicago Fire of 1871, which wiped out the family's extensive real estate investments. When Moody and his music associate, Ira Sankey, left for Great Britain for an evangelistic campaign, Spafford decided to lift the spirits of his family by taking them on a vacation to Europe. He also planned to assist in the Moody-Sankey meetings there.

In November 1873, Spafford was detained by urgent business, but he sent his wife and four daughters as scheduled on the SS *Ville du Harve*, planning to join them soon. Halfway across the Atlantic, the ship was struck by an English vessel and sank in twelve minutes. All four of the Spafford daughters—Tanetta, Maggie, Annie, and Bessie—were among the 226 who drowned. Mrs. Spafford was among the few who were miraculously saved.

Horatio Spafford stood hour after hour on the deck of the ship that was carrying him to join his grieving wife in Cardiff, Wales.

When the ship passed the approximate place where his precious daughters had drowned, Spafford received sustaining comfort from God that enabled him to write, "When sorrows like sea billows roll . . . It is well with my soul."

What a picture of our hope!

LIVING THE MELODY

Ask yourself if you can truthfully say, "It is well with my soul," no matter the circumstances surrounding you. It's absolutely acceptable if you are not there yet. Life is a process. Today choose to say with the psalmist, "I am trusting you, O LORD, saying, 'You are my God!'" (Psalm 31:14 NLT). Then write down some ways God has fulfilled his promises in your life.

What Scripture Says

When I am overwhelmed,
  you alone know the way I should turn. . . .
Then I pray to you, O LORD.
  I say, "You are my place of refuge.
  You are all I really want in life."
—Psalm 142:3, 5 NLT

We also glory in our sufferings, because we know that suffering produces perseverance; perseverance, character; and character, hope. And hope does not put us to shame, because God's love has been poured out into our hearts through the Holy Spirit, who has been given to us.
—Romans 5:3–5

Wisdom from History

Believe God's love and power more than you believe your own feelings and experiences. Your rock is Christ, and it is not the rock that ebbs and flows but the sea.[40]
—Samuel Rutherford (ca. 1600–1661)

Rutherford was a Scottish pastor, theologian, and author in the seventeenth century. He was prohibited from preaching and exiled to the town of Aberdeen, where he wrote many of the letters he is best known for.

Application Questions

- Have you had a time in your life when sorrows like sea billows rolled? If so, how did you deal with the struggle?
- What are some of the reasons Spafford offers regarding why it was well with his soul? What reasons would you add?

NOTES

1. "Original Letter from the Rev. R. Robinson, Late of Cambridge, to the Rev. G. Whitefield," *The Evangelical Magazine* 11 (1803): 331.
2. *Julian of Norwich: Revelations of Divine Love*, trans. Elizabeth Spearing (New York: Penguin Classics, 1998), chap. 5.
3. Charles H. Gabriel, *The Singers and Their Songs: Sketches of Living Gospel Hymn Writers* (Chicago: Rodeheaver, 1916), 22.
4. J. H. Merle D'Aubigne, *History of the Reformation in the Sixteenth Century*, vol. 4 (Glasgow: William Collins, Sons, 1866), 152.
5. Martin H. Manser, comp., *The Westminster Collection of Christian Quotations* (Louisville, KY: Westminster John Knox, 2001), 153.
6. Lorenzo Scupoli, *Unseen Warfare: The Spiritual Combat and Path to Paradise of Lorenzo Scupoli*, ed. Nicodemus of the Holy Mountain, rev. Theophan the Recluse, trans. E. Kadloubovsky and G. E. H. Palmer (Crestwood, NY: St. Vladimir's Seminary Press, 1987), 85.
7. Frank W. Boreham, *A Bunch of Everlastings: Or Texts That Made History, A Volume of Sermons* (London: The Epworth Press, 1920), 231.
8. Thomas á Kempis, *The Imitation of Christ*, trans. Aloysius Croft and Harold Bolton (Mineola, NY: Dover, 2003), 38.
9. Benedicta Ward, trans., *The Sayings of the Desert Fathers: The Alphabetical Collection*, rev. ed. (Trappist, KY: Cistercian, 1984), s.vv. "Anthony the Great, 9."
10. Samuel Medley, *Hymns: The Public Worship and Private Devotions of True Christians Assisted, in Some Thoughts in Verse* (London: Luke Hansard, 1800), iii.

11. John Gadsby, *Memoirs of the Principle Hymn-Writers & Compilers of the 17th, 18th, & 19th Centuries*, 3rd ed. (London: John Gadsby, 1861), 95.

12. Matthew Levering, ed., *On Prayer and Contemplation: Classic and Contemporary Texts* (New York: Sheed & Ward, 2005), 28.

13. St. Basil the Great, "Homily V," in *St. Basil: Letters and Select Works*, vol. 8 in *A Select Library of Nicene and Post-Nicene Fathers of the Christian Church*, 2nd ser., ed. Philip Schaff and Henry Wace (New York: The Christian Literature Company, 1895).

14. C. S. Lewis, *Letters to an American Lady* (Grand Rapids: Eerdmans, 2014), 87.

15. Justin Taylor, "G. K. Chesterton on Gratitude and Thanksgiving," *The Gospel Coalition* (blog), November 26, 2015, www.the gospelcoalition.org/blogs/justin-taylor/6-quotes-from-g-k -chesterton-on-gratitude-and-thanksgiving.

16. "Ambrose of Milan," *Christianity Today*, accessed October 3, 2023, www.christianitytoday.com/history/people/pastorsand preachers/ambrose-of-milan.html.

17. Karl Barth, *Church Dogmatics*, vol. 3, part 4 (Edinburgh: T & T Clark, 1961), 376.

18. Ward, *The Sayings of the Desert Fathers*, s.vv. "Poemen (Called the Shepherd), 53."

19. Moseley H. Williams, "Applications and Illustrations," in "Lesson VIII, The Man Born Blind," *The Sunday School World* 40, no. 8 (August 1900): 302.

20. Samuel Taylor Coleridge, *Aids to Reflection*, 4th ed. (London: William Pickering, 1839), 146.

21. Francis Bacon, quoted in *Forty Thousand Sublime and Beautiful Thoughts Gathered from the Roses, Clover Blossoms, Geraniums, Violets, Morning-glories, and Pansies of Literature*, comp. Charles Noel Douglas (New York: The Christian Herald, 1915), 173.

22. *Charles Wesley: A Reader*, ed. John R. Tyson (New York: Oxford University Press, 1989), 100.

23. Saint Isaac the Syrian, "Homily 56," in *The Ascetical Homilies of Saint Isaac the Syrian* (Boston: Holy Transfiguration Monastery, 1984), 89.

24. Charles Haddon Spurgeon, "A Happy Christian," *Metropolitan Tabernacle Pulpit* 13 (1867), accessed May 2, 2024, www.spurgeon.org/resource-library/sermons/a-happy-christian/#flipbook.

25. Watchman Nee, *Journeying Towards the Spiritual: A Digest of the Spiritual Man* (Richmond, VA: Christian Fellowship, 2006), 146.

26. William Young Fullerton, *C. H. Spurgeon: A Biography* (London: Williams and Norgate, 1920), 281.

27. Charles H. Spurgeon, *The Treasury of David: Spurgeon's Classic Work on the Psalms Abridged in One Volume*, abr. David O. Fuller (Grand Rapids: Kregel, 1976), 107.

28. Thomas Merton, *Thoughts in Solitude* (New York: Farrar, Straus and Giroux, 1999), 33.

29. Isaac Watts, *Hymns and Spiritual Songs* (Birmingham, England: Thomas Pearson, 1791), i.

30. A. W. Tozer, *The Pursuit of God* (Christian Publications, 1948; Project Gutenberg, 2008), www.gutenberg.org/files/25141/25141-h/25141-h.htm#:—:text=God%20is%20a%20Person%2C%20and,our%20wills%20and%20our%20emotions.

31. Elisabeth Elliot, *The Path of Loneliness: Finding Your Way Through the Wilderness to God* (Grand Rapids: Revell, 2007), 128.

32. Henri Nouwen, *The Road to Daybreak: A Spiritual Journey* (New York: Crown, 1990), 9.

33. Amy Carmichael, *Edges of His Ways: Daily Devotional Notes* (Fort Washington, PA: CLC Publications, 2011), 17.

34. Dorothy L. Sayers, *Christian Letters to a Post-Christian World:*

A Selection of Essays, ed. Roderick Jellema (Grand Rapids: Eerdmans, 1969), 16.

35. Benedicta Ward, trans., *The Wisdom of the Desert Fathers* (Oxford: SLG Press, 1975), s.vv. "82."

36. George MacDonald, *God's Words to His Children: Sermons Spoken and Unspoken* (New York: Funk & Wagnalls, 1887), 106.

37. Richard J. Foster and James Bryan Smith, eds., *Devotional Classics: Selected Readings for Individuals and Groups*, rev. ed. (New York: HarperOne, 2005), 372.

38. Saint Augustine, quoted in Eugene H. Peterson, *God's Message for Each Day: Wisdom from the Word of God* (Nashville: Thomas Nelson, 2004), 227.

39. G. E. H. Palmer, Philip Sherrard, and Kallistos Ware, trans. and eds., *The Philokalia: The Complete Text*, vol. 4 (London: Faber and Faber, 1995), 316.

40. Harvest House Publishers, *KJV Devotional for Men* (Eugene, OR: Harvest House, 2022), 163.

SELECTED BIBLIOGRAPHY

Bailey, Albert B. *The Gospel in Hymns*, New York: Charles Scribner's Sons, 1950.

Barrows, Cliff, ed. *Crusade Hymn Stories*. Chicago: Hope Publishing, 1967.

Benson, Louis F. *The English Hymn*. New York: George H. Doran, 1915. Reprint, Richmond, VA: John Knox, 1962.

Blanchard, Kathleen. *Stories of Favorite Hymns*. Grand Rapids: Zondervan, 1940.

Brown, Theron, and Hezekiah Butterworth. *The Story of the Hymns and Tunes*. New York: George H. Doran, 1906.

Clark, W. Thorburn. *Stories of Fadeless Hymns*. Nashville: Broadman, 1949.

Davies, James P. *Sing with Understanding*. Chicago: Covenant, 1966.

Douglas, Charles W. *Church Music in History and Practice*. New York: Charles Scribner's Sons, 1937. Revised 1962 by Leonard Ellinwood.

Emurian, Ernest K. *Living Stories of Famous Hymns*. Boston: W. A. Wilde, 1955.

Erickson, J. Irving. *Twice-Born Hymns*. Chicago: Covenant, 1976.

Frost, Maurice. *Historical Companion to Hymns Ancient and Modern*. London: William Clowes and Sons, 1962.

Gabriel, C. H. *The Singers and Their Songs*. Winona Lake, IN: Rodeheaver, 1915.

Hagedorn, Ivan H. *Stories of Great Hymn Writers*. Grand Rapids: Zondervan, 1948.

Hustad, Donald P. *Hymns for the Living Church*. Carol Stream, IL: Hope Publishing, 1978.

————. *Dictionary-Handbook to Hymns for the Living Church*. Carol Stream, IL: Hope Publishing.

————. *Jubilate! Church Music in the Evangelical Tradition.* Carol Stream, IL: Hope Publishing.

Julian, John. *A Dictionary of Hymnology.* 2 volumes. New York: Charles Scribner's Sons, 1892. Reprint, Grand Rapids: Kregel, 1985.

Kerr, Phil. *Music in Evangelism and Stories of Famous Christian Songs.* Glendale, CA: Gospel Music Publishers, 1939.

Lillenas, Haldor. *Modern Gospel Song Stories.* Kansas City, MO: Lillenas, 1952.

Loewen, Alice, Harold Moyer, and Mary Oyer. *Exploring the Mennonite Hymnal: Handbook.* Newton, KS: Faith and Life, 1983.

Marks, Harvey B. *The Rise and Growth of English Hymnody.* New York: Fleming H. Revell, 1938.

McCutchan, Robert G. *Hymn Tune Names, Their Sources and Significance.* New York: Abingdon, 1957.

————. *Our Hymnody: A Manual of the Methodist Hymnal,* 2nd ed. New York and Nashville: Abingdon-Cokesbury, 1942.

Peterson, John W. *The Miracle Goes On.* Grand Rapids: Zondervan, 1976.

Reynolds, William J., and Milburn Price. *A Joyful Sound: Christian Hymnody.* New York: Holt, Rinehart and Winston, 1978.

Reynolds, William J. *Hymns of Our Faith, A Handbook for the Baptist Hymnal.* Nashville: Broadman, 1964.

————. *Companion to the Baptist Hymnal.* Nashville: Broadman, 1976.

Routley, Erik. *Hymns Today and Tomorrow.* New York: Abingdon, 1964.

Routley, Erik. *Hymns and the Faith.* Grand Rapids: Eerdmans, 1968.

Rudin, Cecilia Margaret. *Stories of Hymns We Love.* Chicago: John Rudin, 1945.

Ruffin, Bernard. *Fanny Crosby.* New York: United Church Press, 1976.

Ryden, Ernest Edwin. *The Story of Christian Hymnody.* Rock Island, IL: Augustana Press, 1959.

Sallee, James. *A History of Evangelistic Hymnody*. Grand Rapids: Baker Book House, 1978.

Sankey, Ira D. *My Life and the Story of the Gospel Hymns*. New York: Harper and Brothers, 1906.

Sanville, George W. *Forty Gospel Hymn Stories*. Winona Lake, IN: Rodeheaver-Hall-Mack, 1943.

Sellers, E. O. *Evangelism in Sermon and Song*. Chicago: Moody Press, 1946.

Shea, George Beverly. *Songs That Lift the Heart*. With Fred Bauer. New York: Fleming H. Revell, 1972.

Smith, Oswald J. *Oswald J. Smith's Hymn Stories*. Winona Lake, IN: Rodeheaver, 1963.

Stebbins, George C. *Reminiscences and Gospel Hymn Stories*. New York: George H. Doran, 1924.

Sydnor, James R. *The Hymn and Congregational Singing*. Richmond, VA: John Knox, 1960.

Thompson, Ronald W. *Who's Who of Hymn Writers*. London: Epworth, 1967.

Wake, Arthur N. *Companion to Hymnbook for Christian Worship*. St. Louis, MO: Bethany Press, 1970.

ABOUT THE AUTHOR

Kenneth W. Osbeck (MA, University of Michigan) taught for thirty-five years, first at Grand Rapids School of the Bible and Music and then at Grand Rapids Baptist College and Seminary. He also served as music director for Children's Bible Hour, Radio Bible Class, and many churches. He authored several books, including the best-selling *Amazing Grace: 366 Inspiring Hymn Stories for Daily Devotions*; *101 Hymn Stories: The Inspiring True Stories Behind 101 Favorite Hymns*; *101 More Hymn Stories: The Inspiring True Stories Behind 101 Favorite Hymns*; and *Devotional Warm-Ups for the Church Choir: Preparing to Lead Others in Worship*.

ABOUT THE EDITOR

Janyre Tromp is an award-winning and best-selling author with a deep love for history. Her books include *Shadows in the Mind's Eye*, *O Little Town*, and *Darkness Calls the Tiger*. Find her on social media or her website, janyretromp.com.